THE PUFFIN GOOD READING GUIDE
FOR CHILDREN

The Puffin Good Reading Guide for Children

Introduction by
Ruskin Bond

PUFFIN BOOKS
An imprint of Penguin Random House

PUFFIN BOOKS

USA | Canada | UK | Ireland | Australia
New Zealand | India | South Africa | China | Singapore

Puffin Books is part of the Penguin Random House group of companies
whose addresses can be found at global.penguinrandomhouse.com

Published by Penguin Random House India Pvt. Ltd
4th Floor, Capital Tower 1, MG Road,
Gurugram 122 002, Haryana, India

Penguin
Random House
India

First published in Puffin by Penguin Books India 2006

ISBN 9780143335078

Typeset in Bembo by Eleven Arts, New Delhi

Printed at Repro India Limited

CONTENTS

INTRODUCTION
Adventure with Books

The palaces, lawns and gardens of Jamnagar, where I spent the first six years of my life, were just the right setting for a child whose first book was *Alice in Wonderland*. Princes and princesses were all over the place, and if the King and Queen of Hearts had emerged from behind the rose bushes I would not have been at all surprised. In one of the old palaces lived a rather dotty old princess who was rather like the Duchess in *Alice*. When I grew up I put her into one of my stories, 'The Room of Many Colours', and several readers remarked that she had walked straight out of Wonderland. And indeed she had. Our first books have a strong and lasting influence on our thinking and the way we look at life.

From Wonderland I travelled to Never Never Land, for my second book was Barrie's *Peter Pan*. Not the text of the play but the book written specially for children. I did read the play (along with all Barrie's works) when I was at school; and later, a young man in London, I went to the old Scala theatre to see the annual Christmas production of *Peter Pan*. That great actor Donald Wolfit took the part of Captain Hook, with beautiful Margaret Lockwood as Peter. I had expected the theatre to be full of children, but the audience consisted largely of adults. Peter, the boy who never grew up, must have appealed to the eternal child in each of us. And when, in order to save Wendy's life, he appeals to the audience to clap their hands if they believe in fairies, everyone clapped, this writer included.

I believed in fairies, I wish I could still believe in them.

Barrie was one of my favourite authors and playwrights. It is not easy to find his works today (apart from *Peter Pan*), but if you come across his other plays—*Dear Brutus, Mary Rose* and *A Kiss for Cinderella*—don't pass them by. They have a certain magic.

In junior school I moved on from Wonderland to the real world, enjoying realistic novels of adventure such as R.M. Ballantyne's *The Coral Island*, Stevenson's *Treasure Island* and Jack London's *Call of the Wild*. But it was only after my father died (when I was ten) that I became a voracious reader. He had been the perfect companion. There was no one to replace him. So I turned to books for companionship.

In my stepfather's house there were very few books, and I had to look elsewhere for my needs. I did not have enough pocket money to buy books, and there was no library worth the name in 1940s Dehradun. But I was to discover some wonderful books in an unusual way.

My mother and stepfather were fond of shikar, and frequently went on hunting trips into the forests around Dehra. On one occasion they rented a forest bungalow for a week, and I was taken along against my wishes. I found these shikar outings very boring. The animals did not have much of a chance—not when they were shot at from jeeps or the backs of elephants.

Resentfully I went along, but declined to take part in the pleasures of the hunt. Left alone in the bungalow, I discovered a cupboard full of books in one of the unoccupied rooms. Here were many authors I had not read before, and I was soon immersed in *Ghost Stories of an Antiquary* by M.R. James, *Love among the Chickens* by P.G. Wodehouse (an early Ukridge story), *The Thirty-nine Steps* by John Buchan, and a couple of Agatha Christie titles. While the shikaris came and went, cursing their luck—for most of the wildlife had already been decimated—I had the time of my life with this little neglected library. I don't suppose it's still there after sixty years. I did not take any of the books when we left, but in later years I went out of my way to acquire these same titles, and I dip into them from time to time. I love re-reading old favourites, especially authors who have a distinctive style or tone of voice—Wodehouse, 'Saki', Maugham, M.R. James, Walter de la Mare, J.B. Priestly, William Saroyan, Thurber, Joseph Conrad …

And, of course, Dickens.

I discovered Charles Dickens in my school library, when I was twelve or thirteen. It began with *David Copperfield* and it would be no exaggeration to say that this book set me on the high road to literary adventure. So closely did I identify with young David that I resolved that I would run away from home and become a writer. I was to run away (briefly) and be a writer all my life.

Dickens's characters, often larger than life, appealed to me, and I went on to read almost all his works. My favourites after *Copperfield* were *Pickwick Papers*, *Nicholas Nickleby* and *Our Mutual Friend*. His descriptions of London's dockland and East End led me to explore these areas a few years later. That London has vanished now, but in the early 1950s, parts of Dickens's London could still be found and recognized.

When I became a senior at school, I was given charge of the library, which meant that I kept the keys with me. Whenever I had a little time to myself, I'd escape to this little world of books, make myself comfortable in a sunny corner, and read anything that took my fancy. It was the only place in school where I could have a little privacy, for boarding schools are not meant for solitary, reflective individuals. I must have read more than half the books in that library. This meant that I did not pay much attention to the subjects I was supposed to be studying; but I managed to get through my exams. And in any case, I had no intention of becoming anything but a writer.

After school, I was packed off to England—or rather, to the Channel Islands, which were part of the United Kingdom. Over there I was terribly homesick—more for India and friends than for 'home'. My office job was drab and monotonous; my relatives, with whom I was living, were unsympathetic to my literary ambitions. Once again, it was a library that came to my rescue—in this case, the Jersey Public Library, where I spent my evenings.

I read everything that I could get hold of that pertained to India—the plays and poems of Rabindranath Tagore, the memoirs of Sudhin Ghose, the novels of Mulk Raj Anand, Attia Hosein and Rumer Godden. I found Rumer Godden's novels especially enchanting—*Black Narcissus* (set in Darjeeling), *The River* and *Breakfast with the Nikolides* (set in East Bengal); her journal *Rungli-Rungliot*, which described life on a tea-estate; and finally, *Kingfishers Catch Fire*, set in Kashmir. I think it was the combined influence of Tagore and Rumer Godden that made me determined to return to India as soon as possible.

But first there were three years in London, where I wrote my first novel; and there I haunted the second-hand bookshops and bought and read almost everything that came my way. But there were three books that always remained with me, and came back to India with me—my *Copperfield*, my *Collected Tagore* (the Macmillan edition) and *Boswell's Life of Dr Johnson*.

My Favourite Books
(over the years)

Alice in Wonderland by Lewis Carroll
Peter Pan by J.M. Barrie
Just William by Richmal Crompton
Adventures of Dr Dolittle by Hugh Lofting
The Incredible Adventures of Professor Branestawm
    by Norman Hunter
The Adventures of Sherlock Holmes
    by Arthur Conan Doyle
David Copperfield by Charles Dickens
Pickwick Papers by Dickens
Nicholas Nickleby by Dickens
Wuthering Heights by Emily Brontë
Boswell's Life of Dr Johnson by James Boswell
Boswell's London Journal by Boswell
The Diary of Samuel Pepys by Samuel Pepys
The Seven Pillars of Wisdom by T.E. Lawrence
Black Narcissus by Rumer Godden
Hindoo Holiday by J.R. Ackerly
The Big Heart by Mulk Raj Anand
The Crescent Moon by Rabindranath Tagore
And Gazelles Leaping by Sudhin Ghose

My Name Is Aram by William Saroyan
My Uncle Silas by H.E. Bates
The Moon and Sixpence by W. Somerset Maugham
The Story of My Heart by Richard Jefferies
Walden by H.D. Thoreau
Kim by Rudyard Kipling
Decline and Fall by Evelyn Waugh

You will have your own favourites, of course, and naturally they will be different from mine. I asked several young readers to tell me the names of their favourite authors. These were their chosen few: Roald Dahl, Emily Brontë, Enid Blyton, J.K. Rowling, Louisa M. Alcott, J.R.R. Tolkien, John Grisham, Thomas Hardy. A mixed bunch, indeed! And it only goes to show that the world of books is rich and varied, and that there are writers to suit every taste. So search for the authors that you enjoy most, and they will be your good companions wherever you go.

Landour
October 2005   Ruskin Bond

HOW TO USE THIS GUIDE

Who is this book for?

If you like reading, this book is for you. The books we read are usually determined by what our friends and family have read and liked, or by what is available at the neighbourhood bookshop or school library. Sometimes this may mean that we don't know about other exciting books that are available. The purpose of this book is to let you know what else there is out there, just asking to be read.

We are fortunate that we are living in a time when some of the best new writing is for children or young adults. You may not have heard of some of these new books and your local bookshop might only have the classics and the omnipresent Enid Blyton, Nancy Drew and Hardy Boys books. If you are looking for something beyond that to read, or if you have specific reading interests, this book should be of great help.

Why do we need a book about books?

Over the past few years, there have been many exciting developments in the world of children's literature. Almost everyone has heard of and read the Harry Potter books, but there have been other equally wonderful books published which are not as well known. Moreover, now children's books are also providing material for the world of films: *Lord of the Rings, Holes, The Princess Diaries* and Lemony Snicket's *A Series of Unfortunate Events* are only some of these.

This book tries to help you to answer the question: What do I read next?

Another reason why we have compiled this list is because you may not be aware of the wonderful books by Indian authors available in your favourite genres.

Does this book list all the books possible for me to read?

This book cannot do that—in fact, it is doubtful if any book can. As there are hundreds of thousands of English books available for the age range four to sixteen, listing all would be an impossible task.

For a start, we are looking only at books published in English (which includes books in other languages that have been translated into English). Secondly, we are looking primarily at fiction—mainly novels, but also some short stories, poetry, graphic novels and comics. There is a whole world of non-fiction and reference material also available for children.

We have tried to list some must-reads in various genres. The choices are, of course, subjective, but they are backed by reputation, awards won and sales figures. We have not divided the books gender-wise, as we believe there is really no such thing as books for boys and books for girls.

Another factor which has been kept in mind when listing books is availability. While it is possible today to buy virtually any book off the Internet, it is still not an option which is very popular in India. We have little access, for example, to books from Africa or Australia. Thus listing them here would be pointless.

The issue of availability is especially important in the Younger Readers category. Many of the books for this age group are picture books, and picture books published in the UK or US are often so expensive that few bookstores in India stock them. Therefore, we have restricted the list to classic picture books and picture books published in India.

How does this book work?

This book is broadly divided into three main sections according to age group:

Young adults: 12 to 16
Middle readers: 8 to 12
Younger readers: 4 to 8

These are merely guidelines and you may find that you enjoy reading books for a younger or older age group. Some readers might find these age group divisions work for them, others not. Reading level is a very subjective thing, which has less to do with vocabulary or intelligence, and more to do with interests. Thus, if you are eleven years old and love historical novels, for example, you might find that you enjoy some of the books suggested as Young Adult historical novels.

Moreover, the difference between what you like reading at twelve and what you like reading at sixteen would be quite vast. Therefore, please treat the suggestions as guidelines only and have a look at the book to see if you think it is something that is right for you.

Sometimes, within a series, the later books might be for an older age group. For example, the later Harry Potter books will probably be enjoyed more by people who are 12+. In such cases, however, the books are listed under the age group of the first books of the series.

The sections for Young Adults and Middle Readers are further divided according to genre. A genre is a category of literary composition marked by a particular form, style or content. Detective novels, travel writing and love poetry are all genres. So, for example, if you like reading mystery stories, you could look up the other books listed in the crime and mystery section.

This genre division is complicated by the fact that one book could belong to several genres. Thus, should the Harry Potter books be listed in school stories or fantasy? They contain large elements of both. Should Gerald Durrell be listed in humour or in animal stories, as his books contain funny stories about animals? Books which belong to more than one genre are indicated by cross-referencing in both sections.

Within each genre group, there are two kinds of entries, both alphabetically arranged. Firstly, there are a number of books which are widely considered some of the best of their kind. There are brief write-ups about the plot (no spoilers!) and their authors, including other books by the author (this is not an exhaustive list, but suggestions up to a maximum of ten books if you should want to read more by that author). Secondly, there is a list of other books in the genre for that particular age group. We have tried to make a balance of the so-called classics and contemporary books.

We have used certain symbols to indicate where books have been made into films or TV serials, so that if you like the book, you can look for the film in your neighbourhood VCD/DVD library. These are some of the symbols used in this book:

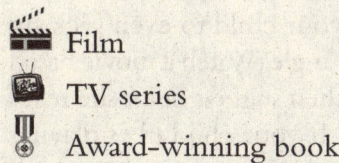

Film

TV series

Award-winning book

What does this book not include?
- Spin-off books from one original book
- Books for under-fours

There are some books that are available in different versions for readers in different age groups, especially the classics and fairytales. We do not list the books available at each level. We list them only in the age group where they can be read in the original, rather than the abbreviated forms available for younger children.

This list is also subjective. If we have omitted any book you feel should have been included, please do write to us and we will include it in the next edition.

Welcome to the magical world of books!

For Parents: How can I help a reluctant reader to read?
One sure-fire way to turn children off books is to try to force them. Reading should be an enjoyable leisure activity, not a chore.

It is good to start with a book in an area in which your child is interested. Thus, if your child likes animals, for example, read about animals. If you child likes sports, then read stories that have sports as a theme. If you persuade your child to read some of the books listed in this book in his or her interest area, we are sure they will become lifelong readers.

If you cannot persuade your child to even pick up a book, go at it from another angle. Watch a movie based on a book with your child, then suggest he or she reads the book to find out more. If your child likes playing computer games, there are many games today which are based on characters and situations from books.

Read with your child (for younger readers)—or read the same book. Discussing a book makes it more interesting. It also helps you to keep an eye on the level. You do not want your child to get bored if the book is too simple or easy, or discouraged if the book is too difficult.

Talk to other people—other parents, librarians or other readers—about what books your child might find interesting, or techniques that work to inspire a child to read.

Once your child shows an interest in reading, allow him or her to pick their own books. Do not force children to read anything—share information, but the final choice should be theirs.

PART I

Young
Adult

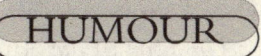

The Thurber Carnival
James Thurber

First published: 1945

In the preface to this book, Thurber writes that this is a compilation of 'the stories and drawings the old boy did in his prime, a period which extended roughly from the year Lindbergh flew the Atlantic to the day coffee was rationed'. It includes such stellar pieces as 'The Night the Bed Fell', 'The Greatest Man in the World' and 'The Secret Life of Walter Mitty'.

To sample just one story, 'The Secret Life' is about a henpecked middle-aged man who dreams of being a dashing naval commander, a heroic pilot performing amazing feats and a daring surgeon who saves a millionaire banker, who has tertiary obstreosis of ductal tract, even after coreopsis has set in … This short story was made into a film.

About the author

American humorist and cartoonist, James Thurber (1894–1961) was best known for his cartoons and short stories published in the *New Yorker* magazine.

Read more by Thurber

My Family and Other Animals
Gerald Durrell

 First published: 1956

From 1935 (when he was ten) until 1939, Gerald Durrell and his family lived on the sunny Greek island of Corfu, moving house several times. The characters in this fascinating and funny book include not only the extremely eccentric members of his family, but also various animals and birds, guests and hangers-on. There are olive groves and tangerine trees, there is Spiro the taxi driver, Theodore the scientist. There are geckos, bats, scorpions, owls, glow worms, ladybirds, fireflies and pigeons. All these combine to make this one of the most delightful accounts of a childhood ever written.

About the author

Gerald Durrell (1925–95) was a famous naturalist, who travelled all over the world to conserve rare animals, and finally set up his own zoo in Jersey, England.

Read more by Durrell

The Overloaded Ark	Rosie Is My Relative
Encounters with Animals	Fillets of Plaice
A Zoo in My Luggage	Beasts in My Belfry
Menagerie Manor	The Garden of the Gods
Birds, Beasts and Relatives	The Aye-Aye and I

The Princess Diaries

Meg Cabot

First published: 2000

New York teenager Mia Thermopolis likes to fit in with as little fuss as possible. Her ambition is to remain unnoticed in her school, the Albert Einstein High School, so that she can have fun with her friend Lilly and daydream about Josh Richter.

All this changes when Mia's father comes to visit. He is not a European politician as Mia has always believed. Instead, he is the prince of a small country, Genovia, to which Mia is the heir. And so she has to be trained for her new role, under the supervision of her formidable grandmother.

To add to the confusion, Mia has flunked algebra, her artist mother has started dating the algebra teacher, the paparazzi have started stalking Mia, and she has developed a strange crush on Lilly's nerdy brother …

About the author

Meg Cabot (b.1967) writes romantic comedies for teenagers and adults. She also writes as Patricia Cabot and Jenny Carroll.

Read more about Mia

The Princess Diaries: Take Two

The Princess Diaries: Third Time Lucky

See also Part I: Adventure

Something Fresh
P.G. Wodehouse

First published: 1915

Clarence, the ninth earl of Emsworth, is on his way to meet the American tycoon J. Preston Peters, whose daughter Aileen is to marry his impecunious younger son Freddy. But what troubles him is that Mr Peters wants to show him his collection of scarabs, and Emsworth has no idea what a scarab is …

Meanwhile, struggling author Ashe Marson is also troubled. His attractive neighbour has just laughed at him, and told him he lacks initiative. So Ashe scans the morning newspapers in the hope of finding an exciting job. Adding to the collection of troubled souls are Freddy, Aileen, and Ashe's neighbour Joan.

So when Lord Emsworth absent-mindedly pockets one of Mr Peters's scarabs, circumstances conspire to bring all these characters (and a few others) to Blandings Castle, where total mayhem ensues as each pursues his or her own ends …

About the author

P.G. Wodehouse (1881–1975) wrote nearly a hundred books. Born in Britain, he lived in the US in the latter part of his life. Apart from the Emsworth books, his other famous series are Jeeves and Wooster, Psmith, Mr Mulliner and Uncle Fred.

Read more about Blandings

Heavy Weather	*Pigs Have Wings*
Blandings Castle and Elsewhere	*Galahad at Blandings*
Lord Emsworth and Others	*A Pelican at Blandings*
Full Moon	*Sunset at Blandings*

Read about Jeeves and Wooster

The Inimitable Jeeves	*The Mating Season*
Carry on, Jeeves	*Jeeves and the Feudal Spirit*
Right Ho, Jeeves	*Stiff Upper Lip, Jeeves*
Thank You, Jeeves	*Much Obliged, Jeeves*
The Code of the Woosters	*Aunts Aren't Gentlemen*

See also Part II: School

Three Men in a Boat

Jerome K. Jerome

First published: 1889

Three young hypochondriacs—George, Harris and the narrator—decide that the only way to revive their failing health is to go on a boating holiday. The only one to object to this plan is Montmorency, the dog, but he is outvoted three to one. And so the elaborate preparations for the trip begin.

This book is a charming, extraordinary and utterly hilarious description of their journey on the Thames between Kingston and Oxford. Not only does every possible disaster overtake them—from falling into a river to getting lost in a maze—but the three friends also narrate stories of their families and the narrator adds his own thoughts on boating, poetic language and history.

About the author

Jerome K. Jerome (1859–1927) worked as a railway clerk, schoolmaster, actor and journalist, and also published several books.

Read more about the three friends

Three Men on a Bummel

Read more by Jerome

The Idle Thoughts of an Idle Fellow

Read more in the genre

DOWN WITH SKOOL | GEOFFREY WILLANS
The hilarious journals of Nigel Molesworth, student of St. Custard's who has a severe spelling problem. The adventures of Molesworth continue in *How to Be Topp*, *Whizz for Atomms* and *Back in the Jug Agane*.

NOTES FROM A SMALL ISLAND | BILL BRYSON
The travel tales of the American writer in Britain.

SCRUFFY | PAUL GALLICO
There is a superstition that if the Barbary apes leave Gibraltar, so will the British. This comic tale describes the efforts of the British army to keep Scruffy, the last and spirited ape alive and well.

RUMPOLE OF THE BAILEY | JOHN MORTIMER
The legal adventures and misadventures of the veteran of the Old Bailey. The series continues with *The Trials of Rumpole, Rumpole for the Defence* and others.

THE LITTLE WORLD OF DON CAMILLO | GIOVANNI GUARESCHI
In an unnamed town in the Po Valley, there rages an eternal conflict between the Catholic priest Don Camillo and Peppone, the leader of the communists. Don Camillo however has a powerful ally: Christ (who answers back). The series continues with *Don Camillo and the Prodigal Son, Don Camillo's Dilemma* and three further books.

See also *The Secret Diary of Adrian Mole, Aged 13³/₄* by Sue Townsend (Part I: Coming of Age), *The Light Fantastic* by Terry Pratchett (Part I: Science Fiction and Fantasy) and *Flashman in the Great Game* by George MacDonald Fraser (Part I: Historical Fiction).

The Catcher in the Rye

J.D. Salinger

First published: 1951

In the fifty years since its publication, this book has reached cult status. This is the story of forty-eight hours in the life of sixteen-year-old Holden Caulfield, set a few days before Christmas. Holden is asked to leave his school Pencey Prep. This does not distress Holden unduly as he finds everything about the school 'phony'.

Holden is quite happy to be returning to New York, but instead of returning to his parents' house, checks into the derelict Edmont Hotel. Here, for two days marked by drunkenness and loneliness, he has various adventures and misadventures.

About the author

J.D. Salinger (b.1919) was born in New York and saw military action during World War II. Salinger mainly wrote short stories.

Read more by Salinger

Nine Stories   *Raise High the Roof Beam*
Franny and Zooey

Doing It
Melvin Burgess

First published: 2003
Jonathan, Dino and Ben are British teenagers, and a subject of preoccupation for them is their sexual development. Dino throws parties when his parents are away, to impress the most beautiful girl in school. Jonathan likes Debbie, but is scared to go out with her because he is afraid of what his friends will say if he dates a fat girl. Ben has been seeing his school drama teacher for a while now.

While the subject may seem outrageous, the treatment is sensitive and funny. The confusions, joys and sexual fears of adolescent males are not a subject many authors have written about, and Burgess handles the issue with great comprehension and sympathy.

About the author
Melvin Burgess (b.1954) trained as a journalist, then worked off and on in the building industry. He has won many awards for his writing.

Read more by Burgess
Bloodtide (see Part I: *Junk*
  Science Fiction and *Lady: My Life As a Bitch*
  Fantasy)

Emma

Jane Austen

First published: 1815

Set in early nineteenth-century Hampshire, the novel begins with the wedding of Emma's much-loved governess Miss Taylor. Deprived of her companion, Emma decides that her mission in life is to marry off her new friend, the orphan Harriet Smith—who does not know who her parents were—to the young vicar of the parish Mr Elton, though her father and their family friend Mr Knightley advise her against it. Harriet, however, likes Robert Martin, a farmer. Hilarious complications ensue, as Emma's plans backfire, and Mr Elton interprets her interest in him as a potential suitor for Harriet to be her love for him.

Emma is the story of the heroine's gradual realization of her own lack of self-knowledge. She wishes to act selflessly so as to bring happiness to all around her, but her efforts are invariably misdirected. As with all of Austen's novels, the cast is small, and the novel is set predominantly in a small village and depicts the life of the community with warm humour.

About the author

Jane Austen (1775–1817) was the daughter of a clergyman. She spent most of her life in rural England.

Read more by Austen
Pride and Prejudice   *Persuasion*
Sense and Sensibility   *Northanger Abbey*
Mansfield Park

Jane Eyre
Charlotte Brontë

First published: 1847

Jane is a young orphan brought up by Mrs Reed, a cruel aunt, and bullied by her children. Eventually, she is sent away to Lowood School, where the headmaster Mr Brocklehurst praises the virtues of poverty, but uses the school funds to live lavishly. Many of the students die when there is a typhus epidemic, including Jane's only friend, the gentle Helen Burns. The epidemic brings to light the abuses at Lowood, and more sympathetic people take over the running of the school.

Jane spends eight more years at Lowood, the last two as a teacher. After this, she takes a post as a governess at Thornfield Manor, where her student is a French girl called Adele. And there she meets the dark and brooding master of the house, Mr Rochester, with whom Jane finds she is falling in love.

About the author

Charlotte Brontë (1816–54) was an English writer, who lived with her sisters, authors Anne and Emily, in Yorkshire. The father was a clergyman. Though she worked as a governess and a teacher for short spells, Charlotte spent most of her life at home. She wrote under the pseudonym Currer Bell.

Read more by Brontë

Shirley   The Professor

Vilette

Paddy Clarke Ha Ha Ha

Roddy Doyle

First published: 1993

It is 1968 and Paddy Clarke is ten. He and his friends rampage through the streets of Barrytown, Dublin, playing cowboys and Indians, etching their names in wet concrete, starting fires and bullying each other. Things are not rosy at home for Paddy and his three siblings. His parents' marriage, Paddy suspects, is falling apart and he feels responsible for this. He tries in his own way to salvage it—he asks questions, so that they will not get into a fight, and he promises himself that he will stay awake all night because he is afraid that if he falls asleep they will argue. He even considers running away so that it brings them together.

The novel is a close and unsentimental look at a young boy growing up too fast and his attempts to make sense of the rapidly changing world around him.

About the author

Roddy Doyle (b.1958) is Irish. He used to be a schoolteacher before he became a full-time writer.

Read more by Doyle

The Van   *The Commitments*

The Curious Incident of the Dog in the Night-Time

Mark Haddon

First published: 2003

Christopher is fifteen and autistic, which means that he has difficulty with certain kinds of things, while being exceptionally talented at others. His mind is very logical, and so it is the illogical—such as metaphors—that confuses him. He is a talented mathematician, and when he is anxious about something, he calms himself by listing prime numbers and squaring the number two in his head.

The novel opens with the stabbing of Wellington, the poodle who lives across the street. Christopher decides to solve the mystery and write a book about it. He plans to use his favourite book, Arthur Conan Doyle's *The Hound of the Baskervilles*, as his model. In the process, Christopher uncovers many secrets about his neighbours and about his own family, and discovers new strengths in himself.

About the author

Mark Haddon (b.1962) is an award-winning British children's writer and illustrator. He spent many years working with autistic children, and this is brilliantly reflected in his depiction of Christopher.

Read more by Haddon

Gilbert's Gobstopper   *The Real Porky Philips*

The Secret Diary of Adrian Mole, Aged 13¾

Sue Townsend

 First published: 1982

In a cul-de-sac in 1980s Leicester lives the bespectacled Adrian Mole, whose life is in perpetual crisis.

The Secret Diary is a hilarious glimpse into the troubled inner life and agonized musings of an adolescent. Along with daily reports of the zits on his chin, Adrian also writes of his parents' rapidly failing marriage, the dog, and his life as a tortured poet and misunderstood intellectual. The others who feature prominently are his mercurial girlfriend Pandora Braithwaite and Bert Baxter, an old-age pensioner who Adrian looks after.

About the author

Sue Townsend (b.1946) is one of Britain's most successful authors of the 1980s and an award-winning playwright.

Read more about Adrian Mole

The Growing Pains of Adrian Mole

True Confessions of Adrian Albert Mole

Adrian Mole: The Wilderness Years

Adrian Mole: The Cappuccino Years

Adrian Mole and the Weapons of Mass Destruction

Read more by Townsend

*The Public Confessions of
a Middle-Aged Woman
(Aged 55)*

Number Ten

To Kill a Mockingbird

Nelle Harper Lee

First published: 1960

The book is set in the 1930s in Alabama, US, where there is much racial prejudice. The narrator is Scout, the daughter of Atticus Finch, a lawyer. The story starts when Scout is six. Her mother is dead, and she and her older brother Jem, make a new friend called Dill. The three children are fascinated by Boo Radley, a reclusive man who they find frightening.

Meanwhile, Tom Robinson, who is black, is accused of raping a poor white girl, Mayella Ewell. Atticus is asked to defend him and is convinced of his innocence. For Scout and Jem, this heightens the tension in an already tense town, and the verdict in the trial can only make things worse. A beautifully told tale, *To Kill a Mockingbird* is about how prejudices do not exist in a child's world.

About the author

Nelle Harper Lee (b.1926) was born in Alabama and spent most of her life there and in New York. This is her only novel.

Read more in this genre

ALL THE PRETTY HORSES | CORMAC MCCARTHY
Sixteen-year-old John Grady Cole sets off to Mexico to forge a new life for himself. The other two parts of the Borders trilogy are *The Crossing* and *Cities of the Plain*.

AT ARDILLA | GILLIAN RUBENSTEIN
An Australian coming-of-age novel about how a new family disrupts the old patterns of the family holiday.

BLACK NARCISSUS | RUMER GODDEN
English and Irish nuns attempt to set up a convent in a palace in Darjeeling.

BORN CONFUSED | TANUJA DESAI HIDIER
The Indian–American experience through the eyes of a teenager.

BREAKTIME | AIDAN CHAMBERS
Ditto sets out to prove that literature is related to life.

CAME BACK TO SHOW YOU I COULD FLY | ROBIN KLEIN
Seymour, whose father is alcoholic, is having a boring holiday with his mother when he makes a new friend.

DADDY-LONG-LEGS | JEAN WEBSTER (ALICE WEBSTER)
Jerusha Abbot is an orphan at John Grier Home who can only go to college thanks to an anonymous benefactor. Jerusha's letters to this benefactor form the story of this witty novel. Read also *Dear Enemy*.

DAVID COPPERFIELD | CHARLES DICKENS
The classic nineteenth-century English tale of an orphan growing up. Also read *Oliver Twist*.

DINKY HOCKER SHOOTS SMACK | M.E. KERR
When Tucker needs a new home for his cat, Dinky Hocker is the only one who is interested. A tale of growing up set in New York.

EASY CONNECTIONS | LIZ BERRY
A famous English rock star falls in love with a brilliant, seventeen-year-old artist who has wandered on to his property to paint. The sequel is called *Easy Freedom*.

FRANKIE AND STANKIE | BARBARA TRAPIDO
A tale of growing up in South Africa in the 1950s.

GOGGLE-EYES | ANNE FINE
A teenager's reluctance to accept her mother's new boyfriend.

GOSSIP GIRL | CECILY VON ZIEGESAR
The lives, friendships and loves of a group of students at a New York City jet-set private school. This is the first book in a series.

A HIGH WIND IN JAMAICA | RICHARD HUGHES
Five English children brought up in Jamaica are hijacked by pirates on their way back to England.

I CAPTURE THE CASTLE | DODIE SMITH
The diary of seventeen-year-old Cassandra, whose family lives in poverty in an old English castle.

I'M NOT BUTTER CHICKEN | PARO ANAND
Short stories about contemporary Indian teenagers.

MILLIONS | FRANK COTTRELL BOYCE
When a bag filled with cash lands at Damian's feet, the Cunningham brothers are suddenly very rich but they have only seventeen days to spend the money.

A ROOM WITH A VIEW | E.M. FORSTER
A young girl's coming of age set in Florence and rural England.

RUN | FARRUKH DHONDY
Tired of being suspected an illegal immigrant, Rashid decides to find his true family.

SUMMER SISTERS | JUDY BLUME
The friendship of two girls over one summer in Martha's Vineyard.

Sweet Valley High is a series created by Francine Pascall, and written by her and a team of ghost writers (many are published under the name of Kate Williams). The series deals with the lives of the identical blonde twins Jessica and Elizabeth Wakefield, who live in Sweet Valley, California, and attend Sweet Valley junior high school. Though identical in appearance, the twins are very different in nature.

The original series dealt with their life in high school. Eventually, however, there were spin-off series about the twins in senior high school (Sweet Valley Senior Year), in middle school (*Sweet Valley Twins*), in elementary school (*Sweet Valley Kids*) and at university (*Sweet Valley University*).

TESS OF THE D'URBERVILLES | THOMAS HARDY
Classic English novel about a young dairymaid in Wessex.

THE CHOCOLATE WAR | ROBERT CORMIER
War breaks out in an English school when a boy refuses to heed the most powerful gang's warning about selling chocolates (see also Part II: School).

THE CHOSEN | CHAIM POTOK
The story of two Jewish boys in 1940s Brooklyn.

THE POWER OF ONE | BRYCE COURTENAY
The tale of a young boy growing up in South Africa, whose dream is to become a boxing champion.

THE SECRET LIFE OF BEES | SUE MONK KIDD
Set in South Carolina, Lily Owens seeks refuge for herself and her companion with three bee-keeping sisters.

THE SISTERHOOD OF THE TRAVELLING PANTS | ANN BRASHARES
The diverse summer adventures of four American girls, bound together by one well-travelled pair of jeans. This is the first in a series.

THE YEARLING | MARJORIE KINNAN RAWLINGS
Classic American growing-up story of the Baxter family in Florida.

TOM SAWYER | MARK TWAIN
The classic American coming-of-age story set in the nineteenth century in the Mississippi valley. Read also *Huckleberry Finn*.

WALK TWO MOONS | SHARON CREECH
Thirteen-year-old Salamanca Tree Hiddle travels with her grandparents from Ohio to Idaho to trace the journey her mother made just before she disappeared.

WEETZIE BAT | FRANCESCA LIA BLOCK
No one understands Weetzie until she meets Dirk, a handsome punk who takes her slam-dancing, beach-hopping and pizza-getting.

WUTHERING HEIGHTS | EMILY BRONTË
The classic star-crossed love story of Catherine Ernshaw
and Heathcliffe.

See also *My Family and Other Animals* by Gerald Durrell
(Part I: Humour)

2001: A Space Odyssey

Arthur C. Clarke

First published: 1968

A monolith discovered on the moon turns out to be three million years old. The *Discovery*, a manned spacecraft, is selected to investigate this monolith for two reasons: its crew is highly trained, and they have a very advanced computer, HAL 9000.

However, HAL's programming has been patterned a bit too closely after the human mind. He is capable of all kinds of human emotional responses—including murder—and he has control over the *Discovery*'s functioning. The crew has to overthrow the psychotic computer in order to fulfil their mission and meet the entities responsible not only for the monoliths but perhaps for the whole of human civilization.

About the author

Arthur C. Clarke (b.1917) is one of the world's best-known science fiction writers, who has won innumerable international awards and published over eighty books. He also laid down the principles of communication satellites. The other famous series by him is the Rama series.

Read more in the Space Odyssey series

2010: Odyssey Two
2061: Odyssey Three
3001: The Final Odyssey

Read the Rama series

Rendezvous with Rama
Rama II (with Gentry Lee)
The Garden of Rama
(with Gentry Lee)

Rama Revealed (with Gentry Lee)

Read more by Clarke

Childhood's End
The Fountains of Paradise
Songs of Distant Earth
Sands of Mars

Prelude to Space
The Deep Range
Earthlight

A Wizard of Earthsea

Ursula Le Guin

First published: 1968

This is the first book in the Earthsea series, which are set in a magical archipelago where dragons are the source of power.

Duny learns magic tricks from his aunt, who believes he will become a great wizard. This is proved when their island is attacked by the vicious Karg, and Duny's magic saves the villagers from certain death. Hearing of this, the master wizard Ogion takes Duny (now named Ged) to be his apprentice.

But Ged wants to learn faster, and so travels to the wizard school at the Isle of Mages, Roke. Though he learns much, he is soon bored and challenges one of his fellow students to a forbidden duel of magic. Ged has not learnt to control his power, and as a result, an evil spirit from the dead is summoned, who attacks Ged and roams Earthsea as a dark shadow. Ged must eventually confront the evil power he has unleashed.

About the author

The award-winning American author Ursula le Guin (b. 1929) has won a worldwide audience with her science fiction and fantasy novels.

Read more in the Earthsea series

The Tombs of Atuan   *The Other Wind*
The Farthest Shore   *Tales from Earthsea*
Tehanu

Read more by le Guin

The Left Hand of Darkness   *Jane on Her Own*
The Dispossessed   *More Tales of the Catwings*
Catwings   *The Lathe of Heaven*
Catwings Return   *Gifts*
Wonderful Alexander and   *The Waylord*
   the Catwings

Do Androids Dream of Electric Sheep?
Philip K. Dick

First published: 1968

It is 2021. The World War has killed millions. Entire species have become extinct and men and women are being encouraged to move to Mars. Everyone who migrates is offered an android slave as incentive. These androids are so sophisticated that it is impossible to differentiate them from real men and women. However, many people choose not to go.

To make matters worse, several androids have killed their masters and returned to Earth. Rick Deckard of the Los Angeles police department is an officially sanctioned bounty hunter whose job is to find rogue androids and 'retire' them. But this is not a simple assignment …

About the author
Philip K. Dick (1928–82) wrote over thirty novels and a hundred short stories. Several of his books have been made into films and TV serials.

Read more by Dick

The Variable Man	A Scanner Darkly
Time Out of Joint	Deus Irae
The Man in the High Castle	VALIS
Dr Bloodmoney	The Transmigration of
The Crack in Space	Timothy Archer
Ubik	

Ender's Game
Orson Scott Card

First published: 1985

Set in Earth of the future, Andrew Wiggin (nicknamed Ender by his sister Valentine) is six years old when he is selected, along with other young prodigies, to join Battle School. The Buggers, an alien species, have already attacked Earth twice within a century, and the children are being trained to fight in case there should be a third attack.

Ender's skills make him a leader in school and he achieves success in the Battle Room, where children play at mock battles in zero gravity. Yet growing up in this community brings with it its own problems.

About the author

Orson Scott Card (b.1951) is an award-winning American science fiction author. He also writes plays for radio and stage. He studied drama and worked as a missionary in Brazil.

Read more in the Ender series

Speaker for the Dead
Xenocide
Children of the Mind
First Meetings in the Enderverse

Read the Ender's Shadow, a linked series

Ender's Shadow
Shadow of the Hegemon
Shadow Puppets
Shadow of the Giant

Read the Alvin Maker series

Seventh Son   Alvin Journeyman
Red Prophet   Heartfire
Prentice Alvin   The Crystal City

Read the Homecoming series

The Memory of Earth   Earthfall
The Call of Earth   Earthborn
The Ships of Earth

Foundation

Isaac Asimov

First published: 1951

This is the first book of the first Foundation trilogy. The Galactic Empire, which has ruled the universe for 12,000 years, is facing a catastrophe created by its own vast size, and seems doomed to crumble to a barbaric future. The only person willing to face this fact is Hari Seldon, psycho-historian and mathematician, who decides he has to preserve humankind's accumulated knowledge. He gathers the finest scientists and scholars, who will embody the hope of future civilizations at a planet at the end of the Galaxy. This sanctuary is called the Foundation. But soon the Foundation finds itself challenged ...

About the author

Isaac Asimov (1920–92) was born in the former USSR but spent most of his life in the US, where he taught biochemistry at Boston University until he retired to become a full-time writer. He wrote over 500 books.

Read more in the Foundation trilogy

Foundation and Empire *Second Foundation*

Read more in the Foundation series

Prelude to Foundation *Foundation's Edge*
Forward the Foundation *Foundation and Earth*

Read the Robot series

I, Robot

The Caves of Steel

The Naked Sun

The Robots of Dawn

Robots and Empire

The Stars, Like Dust

The Currents of Space

Pebble in the Sky

Read more by Asimov

Fantastic Voyage

Fantastic Voyage II

Nemesis

The Gods Themselves

The End of Eternity

The Amulet of Samarkand
Jonathan Stroud

First published: 2003
This is the first part of the Bartimaeus trilogy. Britain and the empire are ruled by powerful magicians. Nathaniel is a magician-in-training, apprenticed to Arthur Underwood, a middle-ranking magician in the Ministry of Internal Affairs. When Nathaniel is publicly humiliated by the ruthless magician Simon Lovelace, he vows revenge. After intensive practice of magic too far advanced for his years, he summons the 5,000-year-old djinn Bartimaeus to steal the powerful amulet of Samarkand and upset Lovelace's plans.

Bartimaeus's sarcastic interjections to the narrative and the copious (and hilarious) footnotes, constantly undercut the seriousness with which Nathaniel sees his mission.

About the author
UK-based Jonathan Stroud (b.1970) worked as an editor in children's publishing before becoming a full-time writer.

Read more about Nathaniel
The Golem's Eye

Read more by Stroud
Buried Fire   *The Leap*

The Fellowship of the Ring

J.R.R. Tolkien

First published: 1954

This is the first part of the Lord of the Rings trilogy. Sauron, the Dark Lord, has risen again and all he lacks to rule the world is the one ring which controls all the other Rings of Power.

This ring has fallen into the hands of an unlikely creature, Bilbo Baggins, a hobbit, who lives in peaceful rural solitude in the Shire. He entrusts the ring to his nephew Frodo, who is then faced with the task of journeying across all the realms of Middle Earth to Mordor, the land of the Dark Lord. For it is only at the Cracks of Doom that the ring can be destroyed and the Dark Lord foiled forever.

This is perhaps the greatest fantasy classic of all time; the book defines the genre.

About the author

J.R.R. Tolkien (1892–1973) was a professor of Anglo-Saxon (old English) at Oxford University.

Read more in the trilogy

The Two Towers　　　　*The Return of the King*

Read more by Tolkien

The Hobbit (prequel to *The Lord of the Rings*; see Part II: Science Fiction and Fantasy)

The Silmarillion
Farmer Giles of Ham

The Light Fantastic
Terry Pratchett

First published: 1986
This is the second book in the Discworld series, perhaps the funniest and wittiest fantasy series in English.

Discworld, the disc-shaped world borne on the back of four elephants resting on a giant turtle of indeterminate gender named A'Tuin, is about to collide with an ominous red star. Eight spells are needed to prevent this; the only problem is that one of them is locked in the head of the cowardly and inept wizard Rincewind, who was last seen falling off the edge of the world.

Aided by unlikely characters such as the Luggage with feet, Cohen the Barbarian and Twoflower, and constantly avoiding Death, Rincewind must make his way back to the fabulous city of Ankh-Morpork. But the way is full of perils, including a stopover at a witch's vacated gingerbread house, a wild ride on a broomstick and a collision with a druid-steered cloud.

About the author
Terry Pratchett (b.1948) lives in Wiltshire, England. The Discworld series currently has about thirty novels (apart from the Discworld books for Middle Readers).

Read more about Discworld

See also Part II: Science Fiction and Fantasy

The Martian Chronicles
Ray Bradbury

First published: 1950

In this collection of linked short stories, golden-eyed Martians regard humans from Earth as the 'invaders from outer space'. The stories describe the first attempts of the people of Earth to colonize Mars, the constant efforts of the Martians to prevent this and the eventual conquest. The tone of the stories varies: some are horror tales, and some comical parables of human folly. Written during the 1950s, at the height of the Cold War and anti-Communist hysteria, they criticize imperialism, racism and the nuclear arms race.

About the author

American science fiction author Ray Bradbury (b.1920) has written more than 500 books and stories.

Read more by Bradbury

The Illustrated Man
Fahrenheit 451
The Golden Apples of the Sun
The October Country
Dandelion Wine
Something Wicked This Way Comes
R is for Rocket
The Anthem Sprinters and Other Antics
Long After Midnight

The Northern Lights

Philip Pullman

First published: 1995

This is the first book of the His Dark Materials trilogy. Eleven-year-old Lyra Belacqua is an orphan growing up in Jordan College in Oxford, England, where she has been placed by her uncle, the powerful Lord Asriel. In Lyra's world, everyone has a personal daemon, an expression of their soul in animal form—and Lyra's is called Pantalaimon. Lyra's closest friend is Roger, a kitchen boy.

Life changes forever when Lyra and Pantalaimon prevent an assassination attempt on her uncle, and overhear a secret discussion about the mysterious Dust. At this time, children begin to go missing, taken away by people known as the Gobblers.

When Roger also disappears, Lyra seizes the opportunity to go with the explorer Mrs Coulter to the Arctic North, where she believes Roger can be found.

About the author
Philip Pullman (b.1946) is the author of several novels for adults and children.

Read more in the trilogy
The Subtle Knife   *The Amber Spyglass*

The Time Machine

H.G. Wells

First published: 1895

When this book was published in 1895, it was considered revolutionary. The Time Traveller travels to the year 802701, where he finds a society of the Eloi, who are beautiful, graceful and frail, and seem to have achieved harmony and bliss. But gradually he discovers that this world is also peopled by the Morlocks, who are brutal and ape-like subterranean creatures. Eventually, forced to flee the Morlocks, the Time Traveller takes off again in his machine, to find himself even further into the future, where he sees a glimpse of a dying world. After this he flees back to his own world.

About the author

The English novelist H.G. Wells (1866–1946) was also a journalist, sociologist and historian.

Read more by Wells

The Lord of the Dynamos   *The War of the Worlds*
The Island of Dr Moreau   *The First Men in the Moon*
The Invisible Man

Titus Groan

Mervyn Peake

First published: 1946

This is the first part of the Gormenghast trilogy. Titus, the seventy-seventh earl of Groan, is the heir to the ancient castle of Gormenghast. The dark and funny tale deals with the first two years of his life. His unexpected birth shakes up the lives of his parents, the seventy-sixth earl and his towering countess, as well as his aunts and the rest of the staff in the ritual-obsessed castle. But in the meantime, the dynasty is threatened by the charming and evil kitchen-boy Steerpike, who begins his ruthless ascent to power.

A mere summary cannot do justice to the power of these books, where the overwhelming vastness and complexity of the castle looms over the weird characters and takes on a life of its own.

About the author

Mervyn Peake (1911–68) was trained as an artist and has illustrated some masterpieces of children's literature.

Read more about Titus Groan

Gormenghast　　　　　　*Titus Alone*

Read more in the genre

ACROSS THE NIGHTINGALE FLOOR | LIAN HEARN
In ancient Japan, young Takeo returns home to find his village in flames. He is saved by the swords of Lord Otori Shigeru and joins a world of warlords, feuding clans, and political scheming. The sequels are *Grass for His Pillow* and *Brilliance of the Moon*.

ABARAT | CLIVE JAMES
First in a quartet of illustrated books about the adventures of Candy Quackenbush in the strange archipelago of Arabat. The second book is called *Days of Magic, Nights of War*.

BEGGARS IN SPAIN | NANCY KRESS
The story of Leisha Camden who was genetically modified at birth to require no sleep. The sequels are *Beggars and Choosers* and *Beggars Ride*.

BLOODTIDE | MELVIN BURGESS
In the not-too-distant future, London is in ruins and the only suggestion for peace is for the fourteen-year-old daughter of one of the rival clans to marry the leader of the other clan.

DRAGONFLIGHT | ANNE McCAFFREY
Fantasy series on an alien world where dragons and humans bond for life, and both are united against the menace of 'thread', little bundles of destruction that fall from space. This is the first book in the Dragonriders of Pern series, which has about twenty books, including *Dragonquest, The White Dragon, Dragon's Eye, Dragon's Kin on Dragonwings* and *Dragon's Blood*.

DRAGONS OF AUTUMN TWILIGHT | MARGARET WEIS AND TRACY HICKMAN

First book of the *Dragonlance* Chronicles Trilogy, which now contains more than ninety books.

DUNE | FRANK HERBERT

One of the most famous science fiction novels in English, *Dune* is an epic tale set in the desert planet Arrakis where Paul Atreides becomes the mysterious man known as Muad'Dib and avenges the ancient conspiracies against his family. The other books in the series by Herbert are *Chapterhouse: Dune*, *Dune Messiah*, *Children of Dune*, *God Emperor of Dune* and *Heretics of Dune*. The series has subsequently been continued by other authors.

ERAGON | CHRISTOPHER PAOLINI

Eragon, the young dragon-rider, and Sapphira, his blue dragon, have to lead an army into battle against the evil King Galbatorix. The second part of the trilogy is called *Eldest*.

THE HITCHHIKER'S GUIDE TO THE GALAXY | DOUGLAS ADAMS

When a cosmic reconstruction team obliterates the earth to build a freeway one Thursday lunchtime, Arthur Dent is saved at the very last second and left to travel the galaxy with his intrepid friend Ford Prefect, a researcher for the revised edition of *The Hitchhiker's Guide to the Galaxy*. The sequels to this comic masterpiece are *The Restaurant at the End of the Universe*, *Life, the Universe and Everything*, *So Long, and Thanks for All the Fish* and *Mostly Harmless*.

JOURNEY TO THE CENTER OF THE EARTH | JULES VERNE

A science fiction classic. A secret message from an ancient alchemist about what lies at the core of the earth makes

Professor Otto Lidenbrock, his nephew Axel and the Icelandic hunter Hans climb down an arctic volcano into a realm of magic and mystery. Verne's nineteenth-century novels of voyages and discoveries make him one of the founding fathers of the genre. Among his other notable books are *Five Weeks in a Balloon*, *From the Earth to the Moon*, *In Search of the Castaways*, *20,000 Leagues under the Sea*, *Round the Moon* and *Around the World in Eighty Days*.

OBERNEWTYN | ISOBELLE CARMODY
After the nuclear holocaust, all surviving mutants are condemned to death or exile at Obernewtyn. Elspeth Gordie finds this a frightening world where the ambitious overlords seek to use the mutants' powers to redicover the secrets of nuclear warfare. The Obernewtyn Chronicles continue with *The Farseekers*, *Ashling*, *The Keeping Place* and *The Sending*.

PRELUDES AND NOCTURNES | NEIL GAIMAN, SAM KIETH, MIKE DRINGENBERG
First in a series of fantasy graphic novels, known as The Sandman books. In this book, Dream escapes imprisonment and journeys to hell to find the tools of power that he needs. The other books in the series are *The Doll's House*, *Dream Country*, *Season of Mists*, *A Game of You*, *Fables and Reflections*, *Brief Lives*, *World's End*, *The Kindly Ones* and *The Wake*. See also Part II: The Supernatural and Horror.

SHADOWMANCER | G.P. TAYLOR
When the evil vicar of a church in Yorkshire tries to overthrow God or Riathamus, two children, Thomas

Barrick and Kate Coglund, join forces with a young African stranger named Raphah to stop him. The sequel to this book is called *Wormwood*.

SHIP OF MAGIC | ROBIN HOBB
The first book in the nautical fantasy trilogy, *Liveship Traders' Trilogy*, concerning the magical ships made of wizardwood. The other books are *The Mad Ship* and *Ship of Destiny*. Hobb's other books include the *Farseer Trilogy* and the *Tawny Man Trilogy*.

SOLARIS | STANISLAW LEM
When Kris Kelvin travels to the planet Solaris to study the ocean that covers its surface, he is disturbed by long-forgotten memories, as are the others working with him.

THE ANDROMEDA STRAIN | MICHAEL CRICHTON
Alien pathogens spread through an American town after a spaceship crashes. Crichton's other popular science fiction thrillers include *Timeline*, *Congo*, *Sphere* and *Jurassic Park*.

THE CALCUTTA CHROMOSOME | AMITAV GHOSH
The adventures of L. Murugan, an authority on Sir Ronald Ross who discovered how malaria is transmitted.

THE EYE OF THE WORLD | ROBERT JORDAN
The first book in the Wheel of Time series. The peaceful villagers of Emond's Field pay little heed to rumours of war in the western lands until a savage attack by troll-like minions of the Dark One forces three young men to confront an unknown destiny. The other books in the series are *The Great Hunt*, *The Dragon Reborn*,

The Shadow Rising, The Fires of Heaven, Lord of Chaos, A Crown of Swords, The Path of Daggers, Snow, Winter's Heart, Crossroads of Twilight, New Spring: The Novel (*Wheel of Time*) and *Knife of Dreams.*

THE GUNSLINGER | STEPHEN KING
First book in the epic Dark Tower series that combines fantasy, science fiction and horror. The other books in the series are *The Drawing of the Three, The Waste Lands, Wizard and Glass, Wolves of the Calla, Song of Susannah* and *The Dark Tower.*

THE LITTLE PRINCE | ANTOINE DE SAINT-EXUPÉRY
A magical fable of love and loneliness, narrated by a pilot in the Sahara desert as he tries to repair his wrecked plane.

THE MISTS OF AVALON | MARION ZIMMER BRADLEY
A retelling of the Arthurian legend from the point of view of Morgaine (Morgan le Fay), who is fighting for ancient Celtic culture as Christianity threatens to destroy it. This is the first book in the Avalon series, written by Bradley and others. The other books in the series include *The Forest House, Lady of Avalon, The Forests of Avalon, Priestess of Avalon, Ancestors of Avalon, The High Queen, The Stag King, Mistress of Magic* and *The Prisoner in the Oak*. Bradley also began the Darkover series of science fiction novels, about the colonists from Earth on the planet Darkover. There are over thirty-five books in this series, written by Bradley and others.

THE RETURN OF VAMAN | JAYANT V. NARLIKAR
A mysterious box containing the secrets of an ancient but advanced civilization is dug up near Bangalore, and three men set out to uncover its secrets.

THE SIMOQIN PROPHECIES | SAMIT BASU

A delightful and funny romp through a world that is at once classic fantasy and its parody. The second book in the trilogy is called *The Manticore's Secret*.

THE SWORD OF SHANNARA | TERRY BROOKS

First book in the Shannara series, where the awakening of ancient evil can only be combated by a sword wielded by the last person in the true bloodline of Shannara. The other books in the series are *The Elfstones of Shannara*, *The Wishsong of Shannara* and *First King of Shannara*. Brooks has also written other Shannara series, including *The Heritage of Shannara*, *The Voyage of the Jerle Shannara* and *High Druid of Shannara*.

THE WEATHERMONGER | PETER DICKINSON

The accidental breaking of the seal of an ancient tomb in Wales sets into motion the Changes, and a brave few have to struggle to prevent chaos. This is the first book in the Changes trilogy. The other two books in the series are *Heartsease* and *Devil's Children*.

THE WHITE MOUNTAINS | JOHN CHRISTOPHER (CHRISTOPHER SAMUEL YOUD)

This is the first book of the Tripods trilogy. Earth is ruled by three-legged machines, and as soon as children reach adolescence, their minds are capped so that they are totally submissive. A group of runaways and rebels seek to free Earth. The other books are *The City of Gold and Lead* and *The Pool of Fire*. There is also a prequel: *When the Tripods Came*.

WIZARD'S FIRST RULE | TERRY GOODKIND

Richard Cypher's father has been butally murdered. The mysterious Kahlan Amnall comes to his forest hideout and they both must face an extraordinary challenge—or die. The first book of the sprawling epic fantasy series Sword of Truth. The other books in the series: are *Sword of Tears*, *Blood of the Fold*, *Temple of the Winds*, *Soul of the Fire*, *Faith of the Fallen*, *The Pillars of Creation*, *Naked Empire*, *Debt of Bones* and *Chainfire*.

THE WOLVES OF WILLOUGHBY CHASE | JOAN AITKEN
Set in an alternate-historical setting in the reign of James II, Sophie, Bonnie and Simon must face wolves and an evil governess. The Wolves series continues with another twelve books including *Black Hearts in Battersea*, *Nightbirds on Nantucket* and *The Stolen Lake*.

WAYLANDER | DAVID GEMMELL
This is the first book in the action-packed Drenai Saga. The other books in the series are: *In the Realm of the Wolf*, *Hero in the Shadows*, *Druss the Legend*, *The Legend of Deathwalker*, *Against the Horde*, *The King Beyond the Gate*, *Quest for Lost Heroes*, *Winter Warriors* and *Legends of Drenai*. Gemmell has also written the Stones of Power series and the Hawk King series, among others.

The Perfect Murder
H.R.F. Keating

First published: 1964

Inspector Ganesh Ghote of the Bombay CID is called in to investigate the attempted murder of Mr Perfect, the secretary of the tycoon Lala. Ghote, who is characterized by his extreme sense of uncertainty and defensiveness has to figure out who tried to knock out Mr Perfect with a candlestick. As there was no sign that the assassin forced his or her way into the home, Ghote assumes the prime suspect is Lala or one of his family members.

Ghote is also facing pressures from his other cases that include a gang of jewel smugglers and some stolen jewellery, and has also to contend with the interfering Axel Svensson, a famous Swedish crime scientist.

About the author

The award-winning crime writer H.R.F. Keating (b.1926) has been writing and reviewing crime books for many years. There are twenty-four other Inspector Ghote mysteries.

Read more about Inspector Ghote

Original Sin
P.D. James

First published: 1996

On Mandy's first day as a temporary secretary at Peverell Press, one of London's old publishing houses whose offices are in a dramatic house overlooking the Thames, a corpse is discovered. However, Sonia Clements clearly committed suicide.

Three weeks later, Gerard Etienne, the head of the publishing house, is found dead, and this is clearly murder. Adam Dalgliesh of the New Scotland Yard is brought in to investigate. Etienne has many enemies— angry colleagues, a discarded mistress and a rejected author—but the puzzle is of extraordinary complexity and the killer is prepared to strike again …

About the author

P.D. James (b. 1920) has written seventeen detective novels to date, many of which have been made into films.

Read more about Adam Dalgliesh

Cover Her Face
A Mind to Murder
Unnatural Causes
A Shroud for a Nightingale
The Black Tower

Death of an Expert Witness
Devices and Desires
A Certain Justice
Death in Holy Orders

The Big Sleep
Raymond Chandler

First published: 1939

Philip Marlowe is a thirty-eight-year-old private detective on the mean streets of Los Angeles. When the daughter of General Sternwood, a Californian millionaire, is faced with a blackmail problem, her father calls Marlowe in to help. Although that assignment is limited, Marlowe soon gets involved with the other problems of the family: the elder daughter faces threats from her criminal husband and the younger daughter is apparently a witness to a murder.

Apart from the resolution of the complex plot, the fun in the book lies in Chandler's writing: the moody central character, the delicate negotiations that threaten to slide into violence and the portrayal of a very dysfunctional family.

About the author
Raymond Chandler (1888–1959) was an American film scriptwriter and novelist.

Read more about Marlowe
Trouble Is My Business   The Little Sister
Farewell, My Lovely   The Simple Art of Murder
The High Window   The Long Goodbye
The Lady in the Lake   Playback

The Case of the Sulky Girl

Erle Stanley Gardner

First published: 1933

Gardner's Perry Mason novels feature the Los Angeles lawyer–detective, his private investigator Paul Drake, his devoted secretary Della Street and Mason's adversary, District Attorney Hamilton Burger.

Frances Celane seeks Mason's help with the problems caused by her father's will. It states that should she marry before the age of twenty-five, the entire estate can be given away to charity. The trustee, her uncle Edward Norton, is determined to stick to the letter of the law. Mason soon learns that his client is being blackmailed. Norton is murdered and Frances is accused of it. The book ends with the usual burst of courtroom theatrics.

About the author

Erle Stanley Gardner (1889–1970) wrote prodigiously all his life. Initially, he wrote short stories. In the 1930s, he created Perry Mason, and began writing novels. He wrote almost eighty Perry Mason novels, as well as other detective novels under several pseudonyms, including A.A. Fair.

Read more about Perry Mason

The Case of the Velvet Claws
The Case of the Lucky Legs
The Case of the Howling Dog
The Case of the Curious Bride

The Golden Fortress

Satyajit Ray

First published (in Bengali): 1971

Ten-year-old Mukul has started remembering peacocks, sand and a golden fortress, probably memories from his past life. When one of Mukul's friends and neighbours is kidnapped by mistake, Mukul's father decides to get professional help. He hires private investigator Prodosh Mitter (better known as Feluda) to escort Mukul to Rajasthan, which is where a parapsychologist suggests Mukul lived in his former life.

Feluda and his cousin Topshe accompany Mukul and the parapychologist to Rajasthan to find the fortress of his dreams. In hot pursuit are some treasure seekers who want to kidnap Mukul.

About the author

Satyajit Ray (1921–92) was an Indian filmmaker and writer. He also wrote science fiction stories for children (see Part II: Science Fiction and Fantasy).

Read more about Feluda

The Bandits of Bombay

The Criminals of
  Kathmandu

The Curse of the Goddess

The Emperor's Ring

The House of Death

Incident on the Kalka Mail

A Killer in Kailash

The Mystery of the Elephant
  God

The Royal Bengal Mystery

The Secret of the Cemetery

The Hound of the Baskervilles

Arthur Conan Doyle

 First published: 1902

Sherlock Holmes and Watson are summoned by Sir Henry Baskerville to Devonshire to solve the mystery surrounding the death of Sir Charles Baskerville. Many generations earlier, the infamous Hugo Baskerville had imprisoned a young country girl in his estates and had fallen victim to a mysterious black hound as he pursued her along the moors late one night. Since then, the family has been plagued by a similar hound.

When Watson goes to the Baskerville family home, an escaped convict is believed to be roaming the moor, in addition to the mysterious death in the family. The tension builds, culminating in a dramatic climax on the moors in the middle of the night.

About the author

Sir Arthur Conan Doyle (1859–1930) trained as a doctor and ran a practice in Hampshire. He wrote fifty-six short stories and four novels featuring Sherlock Holmes.

Read more about Sherlock Holmes

A Study in Scarlet
The Sign of the Four
The Adventures of Sherlock Holmes
The Memoirs of Sherlock Holmes

The Return of Sherlock Holmes
The Valley of Fear
His Last Bow
The Case-Book of Sherlock Holmes

The Murder of Roger Ackroyd
Agatha Christie

First published: 1926
This is one of the earliest Hercule Poirot mysteries in order of writing, though Poirot is shown to be retired.

In the quiet English village of King's Abbot, where Hercule Poirot has retired to grow vegetable marrows, a widow's suicide gives rise to suspicion and gossip. People say that Mrs Ferrars murdered her first husband, that she was being blackmailed and that her secret lover was Roger Ackroyd. Then Ackroyd is found murdered.

There is a full cast of characters in the usual Christie style, all of whom have something to gain from Ackroyd's death, and the surprise ending turns the genre on its head.

About the author
Agatha Christie (1890–1975) wrote seventy-nine crime novels and short story collections, over a dozen plays (including *The Mousetrap*, which is now the longest continuously running play in theatrical history) as well as romantic novels and non-fiction. The other famous detective created by her is Miss Marple.

Read more about Hercule Poirot
The Mystery of the Blue Train
Peril at End House
Murder on the Orient Express
Cards on the Table
Death on the Nile

Murder in the Mews   The Hollow
Appointment with Death   Cat among the Pigeons
Five Little Pigs

Read about Miss Marple

4.50 from Paddington   A Murder Is Announced
The Mirror Crack'd from   Murder at the Vicarage
  Side to Side   A Pocket Full of Rye
Miss Marple's Final Cases   Sleeping Murder
  and Two Other Stories   They Do It with Mirrors
The Moving Finger   The Thirteen Problems

The No. 1 Ladies Detective Agency
Alexander McCall Smith

First published: 1998

Precious Ramotswe is a most unusual detective. When she sets up the first women's detective agency in Botswana to 'help people with problems in their lives', it is a small commercial enterprise. But soon it becomes somewhat a legend.

In this first book of the series, she is asked to find a missing husband, uncover a con man, and follow a wayward daughter. But the case that moves her most deeply and puts her in dangerous situations is that of a missing eleven-year-old boy, who may have been snatched by witch doctors.

About the author

Scotland-based Alexander McCall Smith (b.1946) is a professor of medical law and the author of over fifty books, including books for children.

Read more about Precious Ramotswe

In the Company of Cheerful Ladies

Tears of the Giraffe

The Kalahari Typing School for Men

Morality for Beautiful Girls

The Full Cupboard of Life

Read more by McCall Smith

Read more in the genre

A GATHERING LIGHT | JENNIFER DONNELLY
A murder mystery interwoven with the story of a young girl deciding her future.

A MORBID TASTE FOR BONES | ELLIS PETERS (EDITH PARGETER)
A Benedictine monk at an abbey in Shrewsbury, near the Welsh border, is the unusual detective in this, the first of a series of detective novels.

ARRIVAL | MICHAEL TEITELBAUM
First book of the Superman's childhood series, which is a tie-in with the TV series *Smallville*. The other books in the series, which are by various authors, include *See No Evil*, *Buried Secrets*, *Temptation* and *Sparks*.

BLACK SWAN | FARRUKH DHONDY
A literary mystery in which an aspiring actress transcribes a manuscript dictated by the eccentric Mr Bernier, which purports to give the origin of Shakespeare's plays.

BOY'S LIFE | ROBERT R. McCAMMON
One morning in the 1960s in Alabama, eleven-year-old Cory Mackenson and his father witness a car plunge into a lake as they complete the milk round, leading to a desperate search for the killer.

DEATH IN KASHMIR | M.M. KAYE
On the eve of Independence, a group of British people gather for their last skiing season in India. Among them is a murderer. Kaye's other detective novels include *Death in the Andamans*, *Death in Berlin*, *Death in Cyprus* and *Death in Zanzibar*. (See also Part I: Historical Fiction).

MYSTERY MILE | MARGERY ALLINGHAM
When Judge Lobbett seeks refuge from the Simister Gang in an island off the Suffolk coast, he does not expect blackmail, abduction and sudden death. Albert Campion, the hero of Allingham's detective series, has to uncover the true face of Simister.

HAWKSMOOR | PETER ACKROYD
Hawksmoor is a detective investigating a spate of serial killings in London in the modern day. But the story also harks back to the aftermath of the Great Fire of London.

SILVERFIN: A JAMES BOND ADVENTURE | CHARLIE HIGSON
A prequel to the James Bond stories, the book features the thirteen-year-old Bond investigating the sinister conduct of a laird in Scotland.

THE BEST OF FATHER BROWN | G.K. CHESTERTON
Father Brown is a Catholic priest who chases robbers, traitors and murderers all over England and Europe.

THE GREEN ARCHER | EDGAR WALLACE
Garres Castle is supposed to have a ghost, who wanders around clad in green, carrying a green bow and arrows. But when a new victim is found with a green arrow through his heart, it cannot be attributed to the ghost. Wallace has written over a hundred detective novels, including *The Green Ribbon*, *The Girl from Scotland Yard* and *The Hairy Arm*.

THE LEAGUE OF FRIGHTENED MEN | REX STOUT
Nero Wolfe, the investigator hero of over forty detective novels, is approached by a group of men who complain of being persecuted by the writer Paul Chapin. A couple

of members of the group have died mysteriously and Chapin seems to be the prime suspect.

THE ROMAN HAT MYSTERY | ELLERY QUEEN (MANFRED B. LEE AND FREDERIC DANNAY)

Detective Ellery Queen assists his father, Inspector Richard Queen of the New York City Police Department, in a murder investigation where the victim's missing top hat is a crucial clue. There are over eighty Ellery Queen detective novels, written by various authors using this pseudonym.

WHOSE BODY? | DOROTHY L. SAYERS
When a body is found in a bathtub, Lord Peter Wimsey is called in to investigate. This is the first in a series of books featuring the aristocratic detective. Sayers also wrote another detective series featuring detective Harriet Vane.

See also *The Name of the Rose* by Umberto Eco (Part I: Historical Fiction)

Coram Boy

Jamila Gavin

First published: 2000

In 1741, Captain Thomas Coram set up the Foundling Hospital in London to provide shelter for abandoned children. Otis Gardinar is known as the Coram man, who promises to deliver unwanted children to the hospital but actually kills them and later blackmails the mothers.

Aaron Dangersfield grows up at the Foundling Hospital, along with Toby, who has been rescued from a life of slavery, and Meshak, who is believed to have saved Aaron's life.

Meanwhile, Alexander Ashbrook, the heir to a large country estate who has been disinherited because of his devotion to a forbidden career, discovers that Aaron is the son he never knew he had. But by this time, Aaron is aboard a ship to America, to be sold as a slave …

About the author

Jamila Gavin (b.1941) was brought up in India and Britain. She has written many books for children, several dealing with multiculturalism. She writes historical novels as well as science fiction.

Read more by Gavin
The Wormholers   *Daisy and the Intergalactic*
                          Travelling Salesmen

The Surya trilogy (see Part II: Historical Fiction)

The Far Pavilions
M.M. Kaye

 First published: 1978

A sweeping epic set in India, *Far Pavilions* is the story of Ashton Pelham-Martyn, an English boy brought up as the son of an Indian nurse to the princess of a minor kingdom. Ash eventually returns to his English family and is sent back to India as part of the British army. Events bring him back to the princess of his childhood, who is now being dispatched as a political pawn to marry another minor ruler.

The book covers the period from the 1857 War of Independence to the Second Afghan War. It is a gripping recreation of a colourful period of Indian history and an epic love story.

About the author

M.M. Kaye (1908–2004) was born, and spent much of her early life, in India. She has also written several detective novels.

Read more by Kaye

Shadow of the Moon   The Ordinary Princess
Trade Winds

(See also Part I: Crime and Mystery)

Flashman in the Great Game
George MacDonald Fraser

First published: 1975

Harry Paget Flashman is a top character in Thomas Hughes's *Tom Brown's Schooldays*, where he is portrayed as the notorious school bully who persecutes Tom and is finally expelled for drunkenness. Fraser's series of Flashman novels are the journeys of the comic hero through the wars and crisis of the nineteenth century. Allegedly based on Flashman's own papers, merely edited by Fraser, these books are a hilarious romp through history.

In *Flashman in the Great Game*, which covers the period 1856–58, Flashman, by this time a colonel, is asked by Prime Minister Lord Palmerston to go to India to investigate unrest among sepoy troops. In India, Flashman meets Laxmibai, the Rani of Jhansi, and later assumes the identity of an Indian sepoy in the 3rd Cavalry of the Bengal Army, just before the 1857 War of Independence.

About the author

George MacDonald Fraser (b.1926) is a Scottish author of historical novels and non-fiction books. He has also written screenplays for many popular movies.

Read more about Flashman

Gone with the Wind
Margaret Mitchell

First published: 1936

The American Civil War is about to begin, but all Scarlett O'Hara, a plantation belle from Georgia is concerned about is how to win the love of Ashley Wilkes. As the war begins and an entire way of life is destroyed, Scarlett's single-minded preoccupation with herself continues until circumstances overwhelm her and the South. With the destruction of Atlanta, a new era begins, where Scarlett has to survive desperate odds and come to terms with a new social order.

Set against the dramatic backdrop of the American Civil War and the later Reconstruction, *Gone with the Wind* is a sweeping epic of tangled passions and the passing of a way of life.

About the author
Margaret Mitchell (1900–49) was a journalist in Atlanta. This was her only novel.

Read more about Scarlett O'Hara
The sequel *Scarlett* was written by Alexandra Ripley. *The Wind Done Gone* is a parody of *Gone with the Wind*, by Alice Randall, written from the point of view of the slaves.

Poldark

Winston Graham

 First published: 1945

Set in Cornwall of the 1790s, this is the first book in the series about the Poldark clan.

When Ross Poldark returns home wounded from the American Revolutionary War, he finds that his father is dead and the woman he loves is engaged to his cousin.

Through poverty and heartbreak, Ross tries to take control of his life, to restart the family tin mines and to counter the challenges of the Warleggan family, who want to take control of that area of Cornwall.

About the author

Winston Graham (1910–2003) was a versatile British writer. Apart from the Poldark series, he also wrote compelling mystery novels like *Marnie* and *The Walking Stick*.

Read more about the Poldarks

Demelza	*The Angry Tide*
Jeremy Poldark	*The Stranger from the Sea*
Warleggan	*The Miller's Dance*
The Black Moon	*The Loving Cup*
The Four Swans	*The Twisted Sword*

The Clan of the Cave Bear

Jean Auel

First published: 1980

A prehistoric novel set in the Ice Ages, about 35,000 years ago. When her parents are killed by an earthquake, five-year-old Ayla is discovered by a Neanderthal group who call themselves the Clan of the Cave Bear, who have been left homeless by the same disaster. Iza, the medicine woman of the clan, nurses Ayla back to health. But the clan sees the little girl as an outsider, who they call the 'Others' (Cro-Magnon). As Ayla grows up, her natural differences cause her to become part of a dangerous power struggle.

This is the first book in the Earth's Children series.

About the author

The American author Jean Auel was born in 1936. Her books are available in over twenty languages. She lives in Oregon.

Read more in the Earth's Children series

The Valley of Horses   The Plains of Passage
The Mammoth Hunters   The Shelters of Stone

The Name of the Rose

Umberto Eco

First published (in Italian): 1980

It is the year 1327. The Franciscan monks in a northern Italian abbey are suspected of heresy. This abbey contains one of the greatest libraries in Christendom, which has not only Christian texts, but also books by pagan, Jewish and Arab authors. However, access to the library is severely restricted.

Brother William of Baskerville, an English disciple of Roger Bacon, accompanied by the young scribe Adso of Melk, is sent to investigate. But the investigation is suddenly overshadowed by seven bizarre deaths, and it is these that William must now investigate.

About the author

Umberto Eco (b.1932) is an Italian professor of language and semiotics, and a historian specializing in the Middle Ages.

Read more by Eco

Foucault's Pendulum   *Baudolino*
The Island of the Day Before

The Talisman Ring

Georgette Heyer

First published: 1936

When his uncle dies, the unromantic Sir Tristram finds himself betrothed to his very romantic French cousin, Eustacie de Vauban. But Eustacie has no desire to be married to him, and runs away to escape him. Her flight turns into a wild midnight adventure that involves a Headless Horseman, disguises, stolen rings, fugitive heirs and murder suspects.

This is a rollicking adventure and comedy, with a cast of delightful characters, and shows Heyer's depiction of the Regency period at its best.

About the author

Georgette Heyer (1902–74) was the British author of over fifty historical romances and detective stories. While the period covered in her historical novels ranges from late medieval to the Napoleonic Wars, her most delightful novels are set in the English Regency period.

Read more by Heyer

These Old Shades
Devil's Cub
Regency Buck
An Infamous Army
Arabella

The Grand Sophy
Cotillion
Bath Tangle
Venetia
Frederica

Read more in the genre

ALEXANDER: CHILD OF A DREAM | VALERIO MASSIMO MANFREDI
The first in a trilogy about the life of the legendary conqueror. The sequels are *Alexander: The Sands of Ammon* and *Alexander: The Ends of the Earth*.

A TALE OF TWO CITIES | CHARLES DICKENS
A classic tale of love and sacrifice set against the backdrop of the French Revolution.

CASHELMARA | SUSAN HOWATCH
The saga of a titled English family in Ireland during the nineteenth century. Howatch's other works of historical fiction include *Penmarric* and the books of the Starbridge series.

FLAMBARDS | K.M. PEYTON
In 1908, twelve-year-old orphan Christina is sent to live at Flambards, a decaying old mansion ruled by her crippled uncle and his sons. The series continues with *The Edge of the Cloud, Flambards in Summer* and *Flambards Divided*.

MILKWEED | JERRY SPINELLI
A vivid picture of Warsaw under the Nazis, seen through the eyes of a young orphan.

PARTHIBAN'S DREAM | KALKI
A translation of the well-known Tamil story of Vikraman, who undertakes to fulfil his father King Parthiban's dream of defeating the Pallava emperor Chakravarti Narasimha Varman to make the Chola kingdom the most powerful in the region.

QUEEN OF THIS REALM | JEAN PLAIDY

A memoir of Elizabeth I, narrating the story of her life in her own voice. Plaidy is the author of about eighty historical novels, ranging from various periods in British, French and Italian history.

> Eleanor Hibbert (1906–92) wrote almost two hundred historical novels. Many of them were under the pseudonym of Jean Plaidy, but she also wrote as Victoria Holt and Philippa Carr. While the Plaidy novels were more directly historical, the Carr ones were usually family sagas, and the Holt novels were pseudo-gothic romances in historical settings.

STOWAWAY | KAREN HESSE

This is the tale of young Nicholas Young, who sailed with Captain Cook and was the first of the crew to spot New Zealand in 1769.

THE PRISONER OF ZENDA | ANTHONY HOPE

A rollicking tale of love, adventure and mistaken identity. The sequel is *Rupert of Hentzau*.

THE THORN BIRDS | COLLEEN MCCULLOUGH

A classic novel of the Australian outback.

TRUE CONFESSIONS OF CHARLOTTE DOYLE | AVI

A nineteenth-century adventure tale of a thirteen-year-old girl in the middle of a mutiny on the high seas.

THE TWENTIETH WIFE | INDU SUNDARESAN

Set in the seventeenth century, the epic story of Mehrunnisa, who would later become Noor Jahan, wife of Jahangir. The sequel to this book is *The Feast of the Roses*.

See also *Captain Blood* by Rafael Sabatini, *Master and Commander* by Patrick O'Brian, *Mr. Midshipman Hornblower* by C.S. Forrester and *The Scarlet Pimpernel* by Baroness Orczy, (Part I: Adventure).

Captain Blood
Rafael Sabatini

First published: 1924

Peter Blood is a seventeenth-century Irish doctor living in England. He is drawn, against his will, into the conflict of the day—a rebellion by the Duke of Monmouth against James Stewart, king of England. However, when Blood aids a rebel soldier who has been wounded, he is arrested and sentenced to death. This is later commuted to ten years of slavery on the island of Barbados. Blood and his fellow convicts are delivered into the hands of the cruel Colonel Bishop, a plantation owner.

However, Blood escapes and embarks on a new career as a pirate …

About the author

Rafael Sabatini (1875–1950) was born in Italy. He was the author of more than thirty novels and several collections of short stories.

Read more by Sabatini

The Sea-Hawk   *Scaramouche*

H.M.S. Ulysses
Alistair MacLean

First published: 1955
This is the story of Convoy FR77 to Murmansk in the summer of 1943. One of the destroyers escorting the convoy is *H.M.S. Ulysses*. On the way, the German military attacks the convoy with U-boats, bombers, fighter planes, a warship, and even threatens to unleash the battleship Tirpitz. One after another, each of the original thirty-six ships in the convoy is sunk.

The book depicts in vivid detail the constant struggle of the men against the enemy and against the bitter cold of the Arctic sea. The action is set aboard the *Ulysses*, and this is the story of the men of the ship and their fanatical devotion to their captain.

About the author
Scottish author Alistair MacLean (1922–87) served in the Royal Navy during World War II. He later became a schoolteacher and wrote thirty-five adventure and action novels, many of which have been made into films.

Read more by MacLean
The Guns of Navarone	*Where Eagles Dare*
South by Java Head	*Caravan to Vaccares*
The Last Frontier	*Bear Island*
Fear Is the Key	*The Way to Dusty Death*
The Golden Rendezvous	*Breakheart Pass*

Hostage!

James Hamilton–Paterson

First published: 1978
Wayne Bulkeley is the chubby, unathletic son of an American oil executive, who is mistakenly kidnapped by a guerilla group in the Middle Eastern country of Zibala. The group's real target was his friend Bernard, the son of a French diplomat.

In the days that follow, as the guerilla group presses its claims, Wayne learns to see life from a different point of view.

About the author

British author James Hamilton–Paterson (b.1941) divides his time between Italy and Philippines.

Read more by Hamilton-Paterson

Flight Underground
The House in the Waves
Very Personal War: Story of
   Cornelius Hawkridge
Gerontius

The Bell Boy
That Time in Malomba
Griefwork
Ghosts of Manila
Loving Monsters

Master and Commander
Patrick O'Brian

First published: 1969

The first meeting of Jack Aubrey and Stephen Maturin is not propitious as the latter introduces himself to the former by driving an elbow into his ribs during a chamber music concert. Nevertheless, the two soon become firm friends aboard the *H.M.S. Sophie*, where Maturin is the surgeon and intelligence agent and Aubrey the Commander.

This is the first book in the series of Jack Aubrey novels, set against the backdrop of the Napoleonic wars. Aubrey's dream is to make a fortune by capturing French and Spanish ships, all of which are bigger and better than his. This is the tale of how he achieves the sobriquet of 'Lucky' Jack, and how the friendship between the two dissimilar men grows.

About the author

Patrick O'Brian (1915–2000) wrote twenty novels in the Aubrey–Maturin series, apart from other novels, biographies and translations.

Read more about Aubrey and Maturin

Post Captain   *The Surgeon's Mate*
H.M.S. Surprise   *The Ionian Mission*
The Mauritius Command *Treason's Harbour*
Desolation Island   *The Far Side of the World*
The Fortune of War   *The Reverse of the Medal*

Smith

Leon Garfield

First published: 1967

Smith is an illiterate young ragamuffin, who lives by petty crime. After he picks the pocket of a stranger, he becomes the accidental witness of the man's murder. Smith discovers that what he has stolen is possibly an important document, and this suspicion is strengthened when he finds he is being pursued by two men.

Smith seeks refuge with a wealthy blind man, who takes him into his home and arranges for his education. But soon Smith finds that he is a suspect in the murder that he had witnessed.

About the author

British author Leon Garfield (b.1921) writes classic adventure tales for young adults and adults.

Read more by Garfield

Black Jack

The Apprentices

Jack Holborn

John Diamond

The December Rose

Devil-in-the-fog

Read more in the genre

AFTER THE FIRST DEATH | ROBERT CORMIER
A busload of schoolchildren become the victims of a terrorist plot.

AUTUMN OF THE ROYAL TAR | BRUCE STONE
When a ship sinks off the coast of Maine, twelve-year-old Nora tries to help the survivors, which include an orphaned boy and an elephant.

THE CORAL ISLAND | ROBERT M. BALLANTYNE
Three English boys, shipwrecked on a deserted island, create an idyllic society despite typhoons, wild hogs and hostile visitors.

KIDNAPPED | ROBERT LOUIS STEVENSON
When David Balfour tries to claim his inheritance after his father's death, he is betrayed by his family and doomed to slavery or death on a ship manned by drunken murderers. Also read *Treasure Island*.

KING SOLOMON'S MINES | HENRY RIDER HAGGARD
Allan Quatermain, Sir Henry Curtis and Captain John Good's adventures in Africa in quest of the fabled mines that are supposed to contain untold wealth. Haggard's other African tales include *She, Jess* and *Allan Quatermain*.

MASTERMAN READY | FREDERICK MARRYAT
The adventures of a shipwrecked family as they struggle for survival on a tropical island with the help of a resourceful seaman.

MOONFLEET | J. MEADE FALKNER
When the fifteen-year-old orphan John Trenchard, who lives in the village of Moonfleet, finds a locket that once belonged to the legendary pirate Blackbeard, his life changes dramatically.

MR. MIDSHIPMAN HORNBLOWER | C.S. FORRESTER

Horatio Hornblower believes that he is a coward but this does not stop him from playing a heroic role in the British naval battles during the Napoleonic wars. The other books in the series include *Lieutenant Hornblower, Hornblower and the Hotspur, Hornblower During the Crisis* and *Hornblower and the Atropos.*

ROBINSON CRUSOE | DANIEL DEFOE

The amazing story of an ordinary Englishman marooned on a deserted island for three decades.

THE SCARLET PIMPERNEL | BARONESS ORCZY

A mysterious Englishman known as the Scarlet Pimpernel smuggles out condemned innocents from France during the Reign of Terror. The other stories of this swashbuckling hero include *The Elusive Pimpernel* and *Sir Percy Hits Back.*

THE SWISS FAMILY ROBINSON | JOHANN WYSS

Swept off course by a raging storm, a Swiss pastor, his wife and four young sons are shipwrecked on an uncharted tropical island.

THE THIRTY-NINE STEPS | JOHN BUCHAN

The gripping story of how Englishman Richard Hannay is caught up in a dangerous race against time to foil a plot to destroy the British war effort during World War I. The other Richard Hannay books include *Greenmantle, Mr. Standfast* and *The Three Hostages.*

THE THREE MUSKETEERS | ALEXANDRE DUMAS

When Edmond Dantès finally escapes from prison where he was incarcerated for a crime he did not commit, he sets out to wreak revenge on those responsible for his downfall. Also read *The Man in the Iron Mask.*

See also *The Princess Diaries* by MEG CABOT (Part I: Humour)

Dracula

Bram Stoker

First published: 1897

The novel is told mainly through journal entries and letters. In the first part, Jonathan Harker, a young English solicitor is travelling to Transylvania to meet Count Dracula, who has recently purchased a large property in London, and to explain the details of the purchase to him. However, his journey to the Count's remote castle is marked by the fears of all those who know his destination, and by sinister events as he nears the castle. The Count is initially a genial host, but soon Harker discovers that his host has very odd habits, and he is in fact a prisoner in a sinister castle.

The second part is largely the journals of Mina Murray, Harker's fiancée, who is concerned about his disappearance as well as the illness of her friend Lucy, who has been displaying strange symptoms. The town is also excited by the strange appearance of a Russian ship where all on board are found dead, except for a huge dog or wolf which disappears into the town.

Dracula is the first major English vampire novel.

About the author

Bram Stoker (1847–1912) was an Irish civil servant who wrote several books of horror and fairytales. He later became the manager of a London theatre.

Frankenstein

Mary Shelley

First published: 1818

The English explorer Robert Walton is on an expedition to the North Pole. One day when the ship is completely surrounded by ice, a man who is in very bad condition is taken on board. As this man recovers, he reveals that his name is Victor Frankenstein and he gradually tells Walton the story of his life.

Frankenstein, who was brought up in Switzerland, was interested in the sciences. After years of study, he was able to discover how to bestow life on inanimate matter—and he created a creature from parts gathered from slaughterhouses, graveyards and dissecting rooms. However, as soon as the monster opened its eyes, Frankenstein realized he had made a terrible mistake. But he had already unleashed a chain of events over which he has no control.

About the author

Mary Shelley (1797–1851) was the daughter of feminist author Mary Wollstonecraft and publisher William Godwin, and the wife of poet Percy Bysshe Shelley. She wrote several novels and also edited her husband's poems for publication after his death.

Misery

Stephen King

First published: 1987

When writer Paul Sheldon is injured in an accident, he is rescued by Annie Wilkes, who is a fan of his. She nurses him, using her secret stash of medicines. Paul realizes that he is virtually her prisoner, through a Colorado winter, bound to do whatever she asks—including write a novel. When he disobeys her, he is punished—his first punishment being two days without painkillers, food or water. Later the punishments get more severe.

It is then that the helpless Paul begins to plan his revenge.

About the author

Stephen King (b.1947) is widely acknowledged to be the master of the genre of horror writing. He has published more than thirty novels, several books of non-fiction and over a hundred short stories. Several of his novels have been made into films.

Read more by King

Carrie

The Shining

Firestarter

Cujo

The Mist

Pet Sematary

Christine

Cycle of the Werewolf

It

The Eyes of the Dragon

See also Part I: Science Fiction and Fantasy

The Boy Who Couldn't Die
William Sleator

First published: 2004
After a friend dies, seventeen-year-old Ken suddenly realizes that he too could die at any moment. To protect himself, he finds a psychic—a middle-aged woman called Cherie Buttercup—who grants him invulnerability from death in exchange for his soul.

To test his new powers, Ken persuades his family to take a vacation in the Caribbean, where he can swim with sharks. But when he begins to have dreams of murders, he realizes that his soul is being used by Cherie Buttercup for sinister reasons.

About the author
William Sleator (b.1945) lives in Thailand and Boston.

Read more by Sleator

The Last Vampire
Christopher Pike

First published: 1994

Alisa (Sita) is a 5,000-year-old vampire but she looks about twenty. And because she has seen most of recorded history, she has many interesting tales to narrate, including how she became a vampire and her meeting with Count Dracula.

Her problem is that her creator Yaksha, who is born from a yakshini (devil), is pursuing her in order to kill her and fulfil his vow to their god, Krishna. This is the first book in the Last Vampire series.

About the author

Christopher Pike (Kevin McFadden) (b.1954) has written over fifty novels. His other well-known series is called Remember Me.

Read more in the Last Vampire series

Black Blood   Evil Thirst
The Red Dice   Creatures of Forever
The Phantom

Read the Remember Me series

Remember Me   The Last Story
The Return

See also Part II: The Supernatural and Horror

The Turn of the Screw

Henry James

First published: 1898

When a group of friends narrate ghost stories to one another in a country house in 1890s England, Douglas reads out a manuscript written by his sister's former governess, who is now dead. The manuscript narrates her experience of working as a governess at Bly, where her charges are the niece and nephew of her employer. Her employer tells her that she must handle all problems on her own and not contact him.

The initial days with her charges, Flora and Miles, are happy, but the governess is soon troubled by the sight of an unknown man and woman, whose descriptions match those of the former governess and her lover, also a former employee, who are now both dead.

About the author

American–born writer Henry James (1843–1916) spent most of his life in Europe. He wrote twenty novels and over a hundred short stories and novellas. Many of his novels and stories have been made into films.

Read more by James

The Europeans   *The Bostonians*
Daisy Miller   *The Ambassadors*
The Portrait of a Lady *The Aspern Papers*
Washington Square

Read more in the genre

BUFFY THE VAMPIRE SLAYER: DUST WALTZ | DAN BRERETON, HECTOR GOMEZ AND SANDU FLOREA
The first book in a series (by various authors) about the teenage vampire hunter that accompanies the TV show. There are also sub-series within the series, focusing on specific characters.

DR. JEKYLL AND MR. HYDE | ROBERT LOUIS STEVENSON
Henry Jekyll creates a potion that can separate the good and evil parts of the human soul. His evil side is Edward Hyde, and initially Jekyll can control the transformations. But after a while, things get out of his control.

FEARLESS | FRANCINE PASCALL
The adventures of Gaia Moore, who is born without the gene for fear. This is the first in a series of over twenty-eight books.

NET FORCE | TOM CLANCY AND STEVE PIECZENIK
The Net Force is the ultimate computer security agency within the FBI, in a world that is now controlled by computers. This is the first in a series of teenage horror books that accompanies a TV series.

PET SHOP OF HORRORS | MATSURI AKINO
The first in a series of graphic novels featuring a unique pet shop in Chinatown, and its owner, the mysterious Count D.

THE PHANTOM OF THE OPERA | GASTON LEROUX
All those who work in the Paris Opera House say that it is haunted. But young singer Christine Daaé's terror is more acute than anyone else's.

SHADOWLAND | MEG CABOT

Sixteen-year-old Suze Simon is a mediator, which means that she has the ability to talk to ghosts. The other books in the Mediator series are *Ninth Key*, *Reunion*, *Darkest Hour*, *Haunted* and *Twilight*.

THE BUG BOY | HIDESHI HINO

Sanpei's only friends are his pets. But when he gets stung by a mysterious insect, Sanpei's life changes forever. This is one of a series of graphic novels by the Japanese artist–writer.

THE CHANGEOVER | MARGARET MAHY

Laura Chant can sense things that others do not—such as her little brother's supernatural illness, and how it might be cured.

1984

George Orwell

 First published: 1949

The book is set in London, largest population centre of Airstrip One, part of the political entity Oceania, which is always at war with one of the two other vast entities, Eurasia and Eastasia. Depending on current alliances, historical records are regularly changed. Meanwhile, Big Brother is always watching you and the Thought Police keeping a check on your mind.

Winston Smith works in the Ministry of Truth, and his job involves the correction of records. Unlike most people around him, Winston's memory still functions. He knows the Party's official image of the world is one that is changed to suit the circumstances.

When Winston finds the courage to join a secret revolutionary organization called The Brotherhood, dedicated to the destruction of the Party, his very life is in danger.

About the author

George Orwell (Eric Arthur Blair) (1903–50) was born in India and worked in the Imperial Indian Police Force in Burma. Later he devoted himself to writing.

Read more by Orwell

Down and Out in Paris and London   *Animal Farm*

How I Live Now

Meg Rosoff

First published: 2004

Fifteen years old and immensely self-assured, Daisy is sent from New York to England to spend a summer with cousins she has never met. It seems like the perfect summer, a carefree pastoral respite. But war breaks out, and Daisy falls in love. And these two events conspire to change her life forever.

This is a haunting book about an imaginary war, which brilliantly conveys how war transforms lives and societies.

About the author

The American writer Meg Rosoff (b.1956) has worked in publishing, public relations and advertising. She lives in London. This is her first book.

Lord of the Flies
William Golding

First published: 1954

A group of English schoolboys find themselves on a deserted island after their plane crashes. At first, the boys work together to gather food, make shelters and maintain the signal fire. Supervising their efforts are Ralph and Piggy.

But soon the order breaks down as some of the boys leave to swim, play or hunt wild pigs. Jack sets up a gang of painted savages. As the trappings of civilization drop away, the boys turn to murder ...

About the author

William Golding (1911–93) won the Nobel Prize for literature in 1983.

Read more by Golding

The Inheritors
Pincher Martin
Free Fall
The Spire

The Pyramid
Darkness Visible
Rites of Passage

The Outsiders

S.E. Hinton

First published: 1967

Ponyboy believes there are two kinds of people in the world: Greasers and Socs. A Soc has money and can get away with just about anything. A Greaser, like him, always lives on the outside.

Ponyboy's parents are dead, and he lives with his brothers Darry and Soda.

When Ponyboy's friend Johnny kills a Soc, Ponyboy's world starts to fall apart.

About the author

American author Susan Eloise Hinton (b.1950) published *The Outsiders* when she was seventeen. Since then she has written a number of powerful young adult novels.

Read more by Hinton

That Was Then, This Is Now   *Tex*
Rumble Fish   *Taming the Star Runner*

The Refugee Boy
Benjamin Zephaniah

First published: 2001

Alem's father is from Ethiopia and his mother is from Eritrea. When these two countries are at war, Alem's father realizes that there is no safety for his son. Pretending it is a family holiday, he takes Alem to the UK and leaves without telling him in the middle of the night.

Alem is left in the hands of the Refugee Council and the British judicial system. This story charts Alem's fate as he is moved from children's home to foster family, and in and out of court hearings.

About the author

British poet Benjamin Zephaniah (b.1958) spent some childhood years in Jamaica, which has influenced his work immensely. His first collection of poems for children was *Talking Turkeys*. Later collections include *Funky Chickens* and *Wicked World!* He also performs his poetry.

Read more by Zephaniah

Face

Read more in the genre

ALL QUIET ON THE WESTERN FRONT | ERICH MARIA REMARQUE
The experiences of a German soldier Paul Baümer, who has to endure day after day of bombardment in the trenches.

A FAREWELL TO ARMS | ERNEST HEMINGWAY
Set during World War I, this is the story of an American soldier Frederic Henry and his relationship with a British nurse, Catherine Barkley. Read also *Old Man and the Sea* and *The Sun Also Rises*.

NO GUNS AT MY SON'S FUNERAL | PARO ANAND
About a young boy growing up in a tension-torn Kashmir.

MISTER GOD, THIS IS ANNA | FYNN
The true story of a friendship between a five-year-old girl and a nineteen-year-old boy.

ATLAS SHRUGGED | AYN RAND
The astounding story of a man who said he would stop the motor of the world, and did.

HOMEWARD BOUND | LAWRENCE BRANSBY
A gripping novel by the South African author about going to school during apartheid.

THE QUIET AMERICAN | GRAHAM GREENE
Set against the growing political turmoil of the US involvement in Vietnam, the story focuses on the romantic triangle between a veteran British journalist Thomas Fowler, his Vietnamese girlfriend Phuong and the American Alden Pyle. Read also *Brighton Rock* and *The Confidential Agent*.

PART II

Middle
Readers

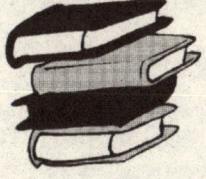

A House Called Awful End

Philip Ardagh

First published: 2000
The Eddie Dickens trilogy began as a series of letters written by the author for his nephew at boarding school. To Ardagh's amazement, not only was his nephew reading the letters, he was sharing them with his friends, and soon everyone was reading them.

In the first book of the trilogy, Eddie's parents catch a disease that makes them turn yellow, go a bit crinkly around the edges and smell of hot water bottles. It is decided that Eddie should go and stay with relatives, at their house in Awful End. The relatives, unfortunately for Eddie, are Mad Uncle Jack and Even-Madder Aunt Maud …

About the author
Philip Ardagh has written more than sixty children's books, including the Unlikely Exploits trilogy.

Read more about Eddie Dickens
Dreadful Acts: Book Two in the Eddie Dickens Trilogy

Dubious Deeds: The Further Adventures of Eddie Dickens

Terrible Times: Book Three in the Eddie Dickens Trilogy

Read the Unlikely Exploits trilogy

The Fall of Fergal   *The Rise of the House of*
Heir of Mystery   *McNally*

Charlie and the Chocolate Factory

Roald Dahl

First published: 1965

There are many stories about Willy Wonka's chocolate factory, which produces the most amazing chocolates. And then, for the first time in a decade, Willy Wonka announces that he is opening the doors of his factory to the public. Five people who find a Golden Ticket in their Wonka chocolate bars will receive a tour of the factory, given by Mr Wonka himself.

When Charlie Bucket finds one of the tickets, he is overjoyed. Along with the other winners, he starts the tour of the chocolate factory—only to find that the stories cannot match up to what really happens within.

About the author

Roald Dahl (1916–90) was brought up in England and was in the RAF during World War II. He has written many books for adults and children. His memoirs are called *Boy* and *Going Solo*.

Read more by Roald Dahl

Matilda

The Wonderful Story of Henry Sugar

Revolting Rhymes

Dirty Beasts

James and the Giant Peach

Fantastic Mr. Fox

Naughty Amelia Jane

Enid Blyton

First published: 1939

Amelia Jane is a wild and wicked doll, whose pranks create havoc in an orderly nursery. In this book, she snips the tail off the pink rabbit, squirts Tom the soldier with a big siphon and gets up to all sorts of mischief at the beach. The toys have their own tricks to teach her to be good, but they never seem to affect Amelia Jane for too long!

About the author

Enid Blyton (Mary Pollock) (1897–1968) has written over 700 books for children, including the Famous Five, the Secret Seven, the Five Find-outers, Noddy and the school stories series.

Read more about Amelia Jane

Amelia Jane Again

Amelia Jane Is Naughty Again!

Amelia Jane Gets into Trouble!

The Bad Beginning

Lemony Snicket

First published: 2001

This is the first book in the series of twelve books called A Series of Unfortunate Events. These are short and extremely funny books about the various misfortunes of the Baudelaire siblings.

When their parents are killed in a mysterious fire, fourteen-year-old Violet, twelve-year-old Klaus and the infant Sunny have to go live with their new guardian, Count Olaf. But the Count is far from being a loving guardian—his sole desire is to get his hands on the Baudelaire fortune and it takes the combined talents of the three siblings to foil him.

If you are interested in stories with happy endings, you would be better off reading some other book. In this book, not only is there no happy ending, there is no happy beginning and very few happy things in the middle.

About the author

According to the books, the author is Lemony Snicket, who was 'born before you were, and is likely to die before you as well'. His 'representative' Dan Handler (b.1970) is the author of several novels for children.

Read more in the series

Where the Sidewalk Ends

Shel Silverstein

First published: 1974

Where the Sidewalk Ends is the land of the impossible. In this collection of poems and illustrations, you will hear of amazing things like the hippopotamus sandwich, the eighteen flavours of ice cream, the dancing pants and the boy who turns into a TV. You will also meet the dirtiest man in the world and Sarah Cynthia Sylvia Stout who refuses to take the garbage out. You will learn how to draw an invisible picture. In the wild, wacky world of Shel Silverstein, anything is possible and the unlikely is likely to happen.

About the author

American author Shel Silverstein (1930–99) was an award-winning poet, cartoonist, songwriter and playwright.

Read more by Silverstein

A Light in the Attic   *Lafcadio, the Lion Who Shot*
Falling Up   *Back*

The Days Are Just Packed
Bill Watterson (text and illustrations)

First published: 1993
Summer is when six-year-old Calvin and his tiger
Hobbes (a stuffed toy to everyone but Calvin) can spend
their day in the tree house. There they can plot their
next move against Susie, Calvin's classmate, argue about
the constitution of the GROSS (Get Rid Of Slimy
girlS) Club and ponder on Calvin's latest invention. This
series has over forty books. Watterson's comic books
have fans of all ages.

About the author
The American artist Bill Watterson (b.1958) is an
award-winning cartoonist.

Read more about Calvin and Hobbes
Something under the Bed   *Weirdos from Another Planet*
   Is Drooling   *The Revenge of the Baby-Sat*
Yukon Ho!   *There's Treasure Everywhere*

Unprincess!

Manjula Padmanabhan

First published: 2005

Meet three heroines braver, bolder and more resolute than your usual swooning princesses of traditional fairytales. On a bus full of princes and princesses, which is kidnapped by a giant, there is Kavita, who can take on his might more competently than any prince can. Then there is Urmila, so ugly that she makes people swoon, who finds more adventures coming her way than any ordinarily beautiful girl. And Sayoni, who has such a power to tame even the wildest nightmare that she is invited to help the President of Sweet Fantasy. Set apart by a freshness and unconventional take on life, these three whimsical, feisty stories are illustrated in the author–illustrator's characteristically bold and quirky style.

About the author

Manjula Padmanabhan (b. 1953) is a Delhi-based writer, playwright, illustrator, painter and cartoonist. Besides writing novels, short stories and plays for adults, she has illustrated twenty-four books for children, including her own.

Read more by Padmanabhan

Mouse Attack   *Mouse Invaders*

(Written under the name Manjula Padma)

Read more in the genre

ABOL TABOL: THE NONSENSE WORLD OF SUKUMAR RAY | SUKUMAR RAY

A delightful collection of poems and illustrations by the Indian master of nonsense verse.

BOTTERSNIKES AND GUMBLES | S.A. WAKEFIELD

Hilarious tale of the lazy, grouchy bottersnikes and the pleasant, squishy white gumbles, and other such creatures from the Australian outback.

FOUR HEROES AND A HAUNTED HOUSE | NARAYAN GANGOPADHYAY

Four friends spend their holidays at a remote bungalow and are plunged into a set of absurd adventures. The sequel is called *Four Heroes and a Green Beard.*

A HANDFUL OF HORRID HENRY | FRANCESCA SIMON

Horrid Henry, with Perfect Peter, his brother, and Moody Margaret, his neighbour, has a series of adventures, which are narrated in this series. The books include *Horrid Henry Gets Rich Quick, Horrid Henry's Haunted House* and *Horrid Henry's Nits.*

JUST WILLIAM | RICHMAL CROMPTON

The tousle-haired, snub-nosed boy has an amazing ability to stir up life in the idyllic English village where he lives.

GOOPY GYNE, BAGHA BYNE | UPENDRAKISHORE ROYCHOUDHURY

Humorous stories of people and animals and their idiosyncrasies.

MOIN AND THE MONSTER | ANUSHKA RAVISHANKAR

The hilarious tales of young Moin who is inadvertently saddled with a monster.

ORDINARY MR. PAI | KALPANA SWAMINATHAN
The delightfully comic tales of Mr Pai and the talking crow, and Bansode the mean landlord.

YOUNGUNCLE COMES TO TOWN | VANDANA SINGH
In a small, sleepy town in northern India, three children gaze out on to a rain-drenched street, waiting for a most unusual guest. The sequel is called *Younguncle in the Himalayas*.

THE SCARECROW AND THE GHOST | KEKI DARUWALLA
Three long, skilful, witty poems with fabulous descriptions of Nature, commenting and reflecting on contemporary issues.

Anne of Green Gables

L.M. Montgomery

 First published: 1908

The Cuthberts of Prince Edward Island, Canada, decide to get a little boy from an orphanage to help Matthew around the farm. But when Matthew returns from the orphanage, his sister Marilla is amazed to find that he is accompanied by a very talkative, red-headed little girl. Marilla is initially reluctant to let Anne stay, but she allows herself to be persuaded.

Anne commits many blunders—she does not know how to pray, she goes to church wearing a wreath of wild flowers, uses the wrong ingredients for a recipe and gets her best friend drunk—but her dreamy good intentions win her many friends.

About the author

L.M. Montgomery (1874–1942) wrote twenty-three novels, over 500 short stories and 400 poems. Like Anne, she lived in Prince Edward Island, and worked as a writer and teacher when she was young.

Read more about Anne

Anne of Avonlea
Anne of the Island
Anne's House of Dreams
Anne of Windy Poplars

Anne of Ingleside
Rilla of Ingleside
Chronicles of Avonlea
Further Chronicles of Avonlea

Read more by Montgomery

Double Act
Jacqueline Wilson

First published: 1996
Ruby and Garnet are twins, and pretty much identical
in every way. Their mother has died, but the twins
lead an exciting life with their father and grandmother.
When their father meets a woman called Rose, they
have to shift to the countryside.

But through all this, Ruby and Garnet bond even
more strongly. Trouble starts when Garnet wins a
scholarship to an expensive school and the twins must
part ...

About the author
Jacqueline Wilson (b.1945) is one of the best-known
British writers for children. She has written over
twenty-five books and has won many awards.

Read more by Wilson
Video Rose
The Mum-Minder
The Illustrated Mum
The Lottie Project
Buried Alive
Lizzie Zipmouth

Take a Good Look
My Brother Bernadette
How to Survive a Summer Camp
The Worry Web Site

See also Part II: Science Fiction and Fantasy

Little Women

Louisa May Alcott

First published: 1868

Set during the years of the American Civil War, this is the enchanting story of the four March sisters: Meg, Jo, Beth and Amy. The father—a minister in the Northern army—is away with the army. The family lives in poverty, but it is a joyous existence enlivened by writing, plays, the girls' various jobs, games with their neighbour Laurie, and Meg's first romance.

But in the midst of this comes news of their father's illness, and when Mrs March leaves, there is a new crisis at home.

About the author

Louisa May Alcott (1832–88) was an American writer. Though she worked briefly as a teacher and nurse, Alcott devoted most of her life to writing sensational thrillers under a pseudonym as well as stories for children under her own name.

Read more about the March sisters

Good Wives   *Jo's Boys*
Little Men

Read more by Alcott

An Old-Fashioned Girl   *Rose in Bloom*
Eight Cousins   *Under the Lilacs*

Malgudi Schooldays
R.K. Narayan

First published: 2002
Malgudi Schooldays contains the complete adventures of Swami, the ten-year-old protagonist of *Swami and Friends* who lives in the little town of Malgudi.

School is bearable only because of his four friends: Somu, Mani, Sankar and Samuel or 'Pea'. But when a new boy called Ranjan joins the group, trouble is inevitable.

Meanwhile, Swami wanders through life feeling sporadically patriotic, breaking windows, catching thieves and missing crucial cricket matches.

About the author
R.K. Narayan (1906–2001) wrote more than thirty books, many of them set in the fictional South Indian town of Malgudi.

Read more by Narayan
Malgudi Adventures   *Under the Banyan Tree and Other Stories*

Rusty, the Boy from the Hills
Ruskin Bond

 First published: 2002

Rusty lives with his grandparents in pre-Independence Dehra Dun. The house is full of strange creatures, like his grandfather's pet python. There are also relatives like Uncle Ken, who impersonates Hallam, a famous cricketer, in order to get a free lunch at a match. Rusty spends his time making friends with an unlikely princess in a lonely tower, encountering a ghost in the garden, and recreating his grandmother's youthful days from an old photograph.

Then something totally unexpected happens and Rusty is forced to leave Dehra, his future uncertain ...

About the author
The award-winning Indian author Ruskin Bond (b.1934) has written over a hundred novels and short stories. He lives in Dehra Dun.

Read more about Rusty
Rusty Runs Away   Rusty Goes to London
Rusty and the Leopard   Rusty Comes Home

Read more by Ruskin Bond
The Hidden Pool   Delhi Is Not Far
Ruskin Bond's Treasury of
   Stories for Children

The Jungle Book
Rudyard Kipling

First published: 1894

Mowgli is lost in the jungles of India as a child and adopted by a family of wolves, who teach him all about jungle laws. His three mentors are Baloo the Bear, Kaa the python and Bagheera the panther. They help him survive in the hard world of the jungle where man-cubs are not welcome, and accompany him through a host of adventures with cobras, tigers and monkeys.

About the author

Rudyard Kipling (1865–1936) was born in India and spent many years there. He was awarded the Nobel Prize for Literature in 1907.

Read more by Kipling

Just-So Stories   Puck of Pook's Hill
Kim   Captain Courageous

Village by the Sea

Anita Desai

First published: 1982

Lila, Hari, Bela and Kamal live in a village called Thul, near Bombay. Their mother is ill and their father is habitually drunk, so the children lead a hard life, especially Lila who has to take care of the whole family.

Tired of their poverty, Hari decides to go to Bombay to get a job. He secures employment in the Sri Krishna eating house, run by a man called Jago who takes pity on the boy. Hari develops a great friendship with Mr Panwallah, the owner of the watch-repair shop next to the restaurant. Through all the hardships of his life there, it is his dream of returning to his village by the sea that keeps him going.

About the author

Anita Desai (b.1934) has written many novels, and she is known for her portrayal of women characters.

Read more in the genre

AN EPISODE OF SPARROWS | RUMER GODDEN
When Angela and Olivia notice the missing soil from the community garden, they have no idea where this will lead them.

ARE YOU THERE, GOD? IT'S ME, MARGARET | JUDY BLUME
Margaret has many queries about life and her changing body, and the best person to talk to seems to be God.

BALLET SHOES | NOEL STREATFIELD
Petrova, Pauline and Posy get scholarships to a dance school and must succeed there.

BLOOMABILITY | SHARON CREECH
When Dinnie Doone is virtually kidnapped and taken to a school in Switzerland by her aunt and uncle, it is an opportunity to assess her life and what she wants to do with it.

HEIDI | JOHANNA SPYRI
Classic story of a young orphan sent to live with her grumpy grandfather in the Swiss Alps.

HOLES | LOUIS SACHAR
When Stanley Yelnat is sentenced to a juvenile detention centre at Green Lake Camp for a crime he did not commit, he finds that the warden wants all the inmates to dig countless identical holes to build their character.

KIRA-KIRA | CYNTHIA KADOHATA
The story of two Japanese–American girls growing up in Georgia in the 1950s.

THE RAILWAY CHILDREN | EDITH NESBIT
When their father is mysteriously taken away on
'business', Bobbie, Peter and Phyllis move with their
mother to a small house in the country.

THE SECRET GARDEN | FRANCES HODGSON BURNETT
When Mary Lennox, a lonely orphan, comes to live at
her uncle's great house on the Yorkshire moors, she
finds it full of secrets. Read also *Little Lord Fauntleroy*
and *A Little Princess.*

RAMONA THE PEST | BEVERLY CLEARY
The delightful tales of Ramona Quinby's first days in
kindergarten. This is the second in the series of Ramona
books.

Alice's Adventures in Wonderland

Lewis Carroll

First published: 1865

As Alice is sitting on the riverbank with her sister, she sees a white rabbit in a hurry and decides to follow it. The White Rabbit draws Alice down a large rabbit-hole, at the end of which Alice finds herself in a long hallway filled with doors. After much difficulty, during which she grows too large to get through the door or too small to reach the keyhole, Alice swims through a pool of water to reach shore with a large number of animals.

In this enchanting nonsensical world, Alice meets a host of unforgettable characters such as the Duchess, the Cheshire Cat, the March Hare, the King and Queen of Hearts, the Gryphon and the Mock-Turtle.

About the author
Lewis Carroll (Charles Dodgson) (1832–98) was a mathematician and writer.

Read more about Alice
Through the Looking Glass

Artemis Fowl

Eoin Colfer

First published: 2001

Artemis Fowl is twelve. He is also one of the greatest criminal minds the world has ever seen. But as the heir of the Fowls—a distinguished clan of international underworld figures—this is hardly surprising.

Artemis manages to decode the ancient book of the 'People' (fairies, sprites, leprechauns and trolls) and decides to steal their allegedly vast reserves of gold. The only problem is that he needs a fairy to do so, and to that end he kidnaps one. Unfortunately for him, she happens to be Holly Short, a tough member of the LEPrecon, a fairy commando unit.

About the author

Irish author Eoin Colfer (b.1965) was an elementary schoolteacher until he became a full-time author.

Read more about Artemis Fowl

The Arctic Incident   *The Opal Deception*
The Eternity Code   *The Artemis Fowl Files*

Read more by Colfer

The Supernaturalist   *The Wish List*

Finn Family Moomintroll

Tove Janesson

First published (in Finnish): 1948
The Moomins live in the far north. After a long winter of hibernation, spring is back. Moomintroll and his friends Sniff and Snufkin can finally get out and play in the woods and fields of Moominvalley. That's when they find the Hobgoblin's hat and bring it back home as a present for Moominpappa.

Unfortunately, the hat is too big for Moominpappa, so they decide to use it as a wastepaper basket. But overnight, the eggshell they have just thrown away mysteriously turns into five small white clouds …

About the author
Tove Jansson (1914–99) was a Finnish artist and novelist.

Read more about the Moomins
Comet in Moominland   Moominpappa at Sea
Moominsummer Madness   Moominpappa's Memoirs
Moominland Midwinter   Tales from Moominvalley

Haroun and the Sea of Stories
Salman Rushdie

First published: 1990
Only three people in the city are happy: Rashid the
storyteller, Soraya his wife and their son Haroun. But
one day Soraya is taken away and Rashid loses his power
to tell stories.

Haroun then sets out to save his parents. Aided by a
water genie named Iff and his mechanical bird Butt,
Haroun and Rashid voyage to a second moon, where
they meet Prince Bolo. But this is only the first step of
the journey, by the end of which they must destroy
the evil Kattam-Shud that is poisoning the beautiful
story waters.

About the author
Award-winning author Salman Rushdie (b.1947) is
the author of internationally acclaimed books like
Midnight's Children.

Harry Potter and the Philosopher's Stone

J.K. Rowling

First published: 1999

Harry Potter lives a miserable life with his aunt, her husband Uncle Vernon and their grossly spoilt son Dudley. His parents had died in a car crash, and he has no other relatives.

However, shortly before his eleventh birthday, Harry starts getting mysterious letters, which his uncle tries hard to keep from him. To escape the letters, the family escapes to a cabin on a remote island. Just as it strikes midnight on Harry's birthday, Harry finds out that he is a wizard, the son of two members of the wizarding community who died to save his life, and that as a baby he had managed to defeat the invincible Lord Voldemort, the most evil wizard of all. And that he is supposed to join, like all other young witches and wizards, the Hogwarts School of Witchcraft and Wizardry.

About the author

J.K. Rowling (b.1965) is the author of this phenomenally successful series. She lives in Edinburgh.

Read more about Harry Potter

The Ear, the Eye and the Arm
Nancy Farmer

First published: 1994
Set in Zimbabwe in the year 2194, the story deals with
the three children of General Matsika—Tendai, Rita,
and Kuda, who are kidnapped, forced to work in plastic
mines and accused of witchcraft. They are pursued by
three mutant detectives—the Eye, the Ear and the Arm.
While in their mothers' wombs, these detectives were
exposed to nuclear radiation, and each has a special
ability, which is indicated by their names.

While the adventure is thrilling, the characters are
both touching and comical, and the book combines
technology, spirituality, military stratagems and folklore.

About the author
Award-winning American author Nancy Farmer
(b.1941) worked in the Peace Corps and taught
chemistry before she became a full-time writer.

Read more by Farmer
The House of the Scorpion   *A Girl Named Disaster*
Do You Know Me   *The Warm Place*

The Incredible Adventures of Professor Branestawm

Norman Hunter

 First published: 1933

Professor Branestawm is the archetypal eccentric English professor who lives in Pagwell. His desire is to create contraptions which will help the community. In these sixteen stories, Branestawm, aided by his housekeeper Mrs Flittersnoop and his friend Colonel Dedshott of the Catapult Cavaliers, creates—among other things— a clock that doesn't need winding, a trap for burglars, a machine that does all the cleaning, and a pancake- making machine.

About the author

English author Norman Hunter (1899–1995) also worked as an advertising copywriter and a conjurer.

Read more about Professor Branestawm

Professor Branestawm's Treasure Hunt

The Peculiar Triumph of Professor Branestawm

Professor Branestawm Up the Pole

Professor Branestawm's Great Revolution

Professor Branestawm Round the Bend

The Hobbit

J.R.R. Tolkien

First published: 1937

In a hole in the ground there lived a hobbit. His name was Bilbo Baggins, and he loved the beautiful world of the Shire that he lived in.

Bilbo is unwillingly drawn into adventure, but when thirteen fortune-seeking dwarfs arrive at his doorstep, in search of a burglar, he has little choice. The dwarfs want to go to their ancestral home in the Lonely Mountains and reclaim a stolen fortune from the dragon Smaug. Along the way, they and their reluctant companion meet giant spiders, hostile elves and wolves—and, most perilous of all, a creature named Gollum from whom Bilbo wins a magical ring in a riddling contest.

About the author

See Part I: Science Fiction and Fantasy

The Lion, the Witch and the Wardrobe

C.S. Lewis

First published: 1950
This is the first book in the Chronicles of Narnia series.

The story begins in World War II England. As the four Pevensie siblings, Lucy, Edmund, Susan and Peter are playing hide-and-seek in a country house, they discover an entrance to the magic world of Narnia through the back of a wardrobe.

Narnia is a peaceful land inhabited by talking beasts, dwarfs, fauns, centaurs and giants. But it has been cursed to eternal winter by the evil White Witch, Jadis. Under the guidance of noble ruler, the lion Aslan, the children fight to overcome the White Witch's powerful hold over Narnia in a spectacular, climactic battle that will free Narnia from Jadis's icy spell forever.

About the author

C.S. Lewis (1898–1963) taught English literature at Oxford University, and later at Cambridge.

Read more about Narnia

The Magician's Nephew　　*The Voyage of the Dawn Treader*
The Horse and His Boy　　*The Silver Chair*
Prince Caspian　　*The Last Battle*

The Sword in the Stone
T.H. White

First published: 1938
This is the first part of The Once and Future King quintet.

The book is a comic rendering of the childhood of King Arthur, or Wart as he is known, in the estates of Sir Ector, set against the backdrop of medieval England. Arthur's education is supervised by the magician Merlyn. In addition to his regular lessons in falconry, jousting and swordplay, Merlyn also transforms Wart into various animals so that he can learn about how different creatures live and think.

When the news comes that Uther Pendragon, the king of England, has died and his heir will be the person who can pull the magical sword out of a stone, Wart's older brother Kay travels to London to attempt this, attended by Arthur.

About the author
T.H. White (1906–64) was a schoolmaster before he retired to research and write.

Read more about Arthur
The Witch in the Wood   *The Candle in the Wind*
The Ill-Made Knight   *The Book of Merlyn*

Read more by White
Mistress Masham's Repose   *The Book of Beasts*

The Thief Lord
Cornelia Funke

First published (in German): 2000

The story begins in the office of a detective in Venice. Esther Hartlieb is looking for Prosper and Bo, who she believes have run away to Venice. Their mother had died recently, leaving them to Esther's guardianship, and Esther had decided she wanted to adopt Bo but not Prosper. Determined to stay together, the two boys had escaped.

Prosper and Bo are in fact in Venice. They join a gang of street ruffians led by the mysterious Thief Lord, who steals from rich homes in Venice to house and feed his group of runaways. Prosper and Bo love being part of this colourful and exciting family, but are soon drawn into darker challenges ...

About the author

German author Cornelia Funke (b.1958) has designed board games and illustrated children's books. She has written over forty books.

Read more by Funke

Inkheart   *Dragonrider*

Truckers

Terry Pratchett

First published: 1988
Masklin and his friends are the last survivors of a warren
of nomes, whose lives are saved when they board a
truck which takes them to Arnold Bros (established in
1905), a giant departmental store. Here they discover
that the others of their race have been living in peace
and prosperity. The store has 'everything under one
roof' and the nomes create their own religion based
on the advertising signs hung in the shop.

But the store is going to be demolished, and so the
nomes have to be persuaded to leave. However, for
many of the nomes who have always lived there, there
is no outside …

About the author
See Part I: Science Fiction and Fantasy

Read more in the Bromliad trilogy
  Diggers   *Wings*

**Read more by Pratchett: the Johnny Maxwell
series**
  Only You Can Save   *Johnny and the Bomb*
    Mankind   *Johnny and the Dead*

Read more in the genre

A WRINKLE IN TIME | MADELEINE L'ENGLE

When Meg's father disappears while experimenting with time travel, it is time for her, her brother Charles and her friend Calvin to rescue him, aided by Mrs Who, Mrs Whatsit and Mr Which. The Time quartet continues with *A Wind in the Door, A Swiftly Tilting Planet, Many Waters* and *An Acceptable Time.*

ALANNA: THE FIRST ADVENTURE | TAMORA PIERCE

First book in the Song of the Lioness quartet. The adventures of young Alanna who disguises herself as a page and wants to become a knight. The other three books in the series are *In the Hand of the Goddess, The Woman Who Rides Like a Man* and *Lioness Rampant.* The adventures of Alanna's daughter are told in the Daughter of the Lioness series.

FIVE CHILDREN AND IT | EDITH NESBIT

Five siblings discover a Psammead or sand fairy near the country house where they are holidaying, and find that it has the power to make their wishes come true. Read also *The Phoenix and the Carpet* and *The Story of the Amulet.*

GLUBBSLYME | JACQUELINE WILSON

Rebecca's new best friend is a 300-year-old magical toad.

HOWL'S MOVING CASTLE | DIANA WYNNE JONES

When the wicked Witch of the Waste turns Sophie into an old woman, she seeks refuge in the wizard Howl's strange moving castle. The sequel is *Castle in the Air.*

IN SEARCH OF WATER | DILIP M. SALVI
Tina helps an alien to find clean water on Earth.

MARY POPPINS | P.L. TRAVERS
Mary Poppins is perhaps the most exciting nanny in the world. For young Jane and Michael Banks, she is the introduction to a world of magic. This is the first book in the series. The sequels are *Mary Poppins Comes Back*, *Mary Poppins Opens the Door*, *Mary Poppins in the Park*, *Mary Poppins in Cherry Tree Lane* and *Mary Poppins and the House Next Door*.

OVER SEA, UNDER STONE | SUSAN COOPER
Simon, Jane and Barney find an old map in a hidden room while on holiday at the Grey House in Cornwall. Along with Great-uncle Merry, they are drawn into a web of intrigue that surrounds an Arthurian legend. The sequels are *The Dark Is Rising, Greenwitch, The Grey King* and *Silver on the Tree*.

PETER PAN | J.M. BARRIE
This is the timeless tales of the Darling children—Wendy, John and Michael—as they follow Peter Pan, the boy who never grows up, into Neverland where fairies live and children can fly. There is a new prequel by Dave Barry to these books, called *Peter and the Star Catchers*.

SEETHU | SHANTA RAMESHWAR RAO
The story of Arun's rag doll, who comes to his aid when his best friend has gone away.

SEPTIMUS HEAP: MAGYK | ANGIE SAGE
Septimus, the seventh son of a seventh son, should be a mighty magician. But he is pronounced dead, just before his father stumbles upon a baby girl … magic and mystery follows.

STIG OF THE DUMP | CLIVE KING

Barney discovers an Early Briton living in the chalk quarry on his grandmother's farm.

STRAVAGANZA: CITY OF MASKS | MARY HOFFMAN

One night when the ill Lucien Mulholland falls asleep in modern-day London, he is magically transported to sixteenth-century Bellezza, a city remarkably like Venice. The other books in the trilogy are *Stravaganza: City of Stars* and *Stravaganza: City of Flowers*.

THE AKHENATEN ADVENTURE | P.B. KERR

When John and Philippa Gaunt, twins living in New York, have their wisdom teeth extracted, strange things begin to happen to them. This is the first in the Children of the Lamp series.

THE BOOK OF THREE | LLOYD ALEXANDER

The adventures of Taran, assistant pig-keeper, set in the land of Prydain. This is the first book in the Chronicles of Prydain. The sequels are *The Black Cauldron*, *The Castle of Llyr*, *Taran Wanderer* and *The High King*.

THE BORROWERS | MARY NORTON

The Borrowers are the little people who live in the nooks and crannies of human houses, and whose worst fate is to be seen. The sequels are *The Borrowers Afield*, *The Borrowers Afloat*, *The Borrowers Aloft*, *Poor Stainless* and *The Borrowers Avenged*.

THE BROTHERS LIONHEART | ASTRID LINDGREN

Scotty is little, but he is also very ill and dying, when his brother Jonathan tells him about Nangiyala, a land on the other side of the stars, where you go after you die. And then Scotty wants Jonathan to go with him …

THE CRY OF THE ICEMARK | STUART HILL
Thirrin Freer Strong-in-the-Arm Lindenshield is only thirteen, but she must protect her kingdom from a terrible invasion led by the winning general Supio Bellorum.

THE DEVIL IN THE DUSTBIN | INDI RANA
When Brum the tamarind-tree devil from Madras finds himself in Wimbledon, all he wants to do is go back home. But Ranjana, the little girl who finds him, thinks otherwise.

THE ENCHANTED WOOD | ENID BLYTON
When Jo, Bessie and Fanny move to the country, they find an enchanted wood with a magic faraway tree on whose branches live Moon-Face, Silky the fairy and Saucepan Man. The sequels are *The Magic Faraway Tree*, *The Folk of the Faraway Tree* and *Up the Faraway Tree*.

THE ENORMOUS EGG | OLIVER BUTTERWORTH
Nate finds an enormous egg in the henhouse, which hatches into a triceratops.

THE KEY TO THE INDIAN (INDIAN IN THE CUPBOARD) | LYNNE REID BANKS
Omri's elder brother gives him a magical cupboard which brings his toys to life.

THE PHANTOM TOLLBOOTH | NORTON JUSTER
As Milo is very bored, when a tollbooth appears in his bedroom, he dusts off his toy car, and drives through to a wonderful adventure.

THE SECRET OF PLATFORM 13 | EVA IBBOTSON
The hilarious adventures of four inhabitants of a magic island who travel to London to find their kidnapped prince.

THE UNICORN EXPEDITION AND OTHER STORIES | SATYAJIT RAY
The adventures and misadventures of Professor Shonku, an eccentric Indian scientist.

THE WEIRDSTONE OF BRISINGAMEN | ALAN GARDNER
On a holiday to Alderley, Susan and Colin acquire the firestone which is needed to awaken the 140 knights of the wizard Cadellin, who are needed to fight the final battle. The sequel is *The Moon of Gomrath*.

THE WONDERFUL FLIGHT TO THE MUSHROOM PLANET | ELEANOR CAMERON
The adventures of Chuck and David who travel in their homemade spaceship to the alien planet Basidium. The sequels are *Stowaway to the Mushroom Planet, Mr. Bass's Planetoid, A Mystery for Mr. Bass* and *Time and Mr. Bass*.

TOM'S MIDNIGHT GARDEN | PHILIPPA PEARCE
As the clock strikes thirteen, Tom opens the back door to find a Victorian garden, where he meets the orphan Hatty.

TUCK EVERLASTING | NATALIE BABBITT
When the Tuck family finds a spring of immortality in the forest, their reactions are mixed.

THE WIZARD OF OZ | L. FRANK BAUM
When young Dorothy Gale's house is swept away in a cyclone, she and her dog Toto find themselves in the land called Oz. She must meet the all-powerful Wizard in order to find her way home. There are another thirteen books in the series, including *The Marvellous Land of Oz, Ozma of Oz, Dorothy and the Wizard in Oz, The Road to Oz, The Emerald City of Oz* and *The Patchwork Girl of Oz*.

When a scarecrow turns up at their cottage to warm himself by the fire, Susan and John realize that he is a very special scarecrow. The other books in the series include *Worzel Gummidge and Saucy Nancy*, *Worzel Gummidge Railway Scarecrows*, *Worzel Gummidge and the Treasure Ship* and *Detective Worzel Gummidge*.

All fantasy books about animals have been listed in Part II: Animal Stories.

Encyclopaedia Brown and the Case of the Mysterious Handprints

Donald J. Sobol

 First published: 1985

Leroy 'Encyclopaedia' Brown's father is the chief of police in a Florida town. But what most people do not know is that his spectacular success in solving crimes is because of the help he gets from his son, who cracks the mysteries at the dinner table every night with some help from his friend Sally. Each book consists of ten mysteries, and the solution is given at the back of the book. Clues are distributed throughout the stories for the reader to pick up and find his own conclusions.

Odd handprints make a wheelchair-bound guest a suspect in the theft of his host's valuables. This is one of the ten challenging mysteries that Leroy 'Encyclopaedia' Brown must solve in this book.

About the author

Donald J. Sobol (b.1924) is the award-winning author of more than sixty-five children's books, including twenty-three books in the Encyclopaedia Brown series. The series has been translated into twelve languages.

Read more about Encyclopaedia Brown

Encyclopaedia Brown, Boy Detective

Encyclopaedia Brown and the Case of the Secret Pitch

Encyclopaedia Brown Finds the Clues

Encyclopaedia Brown Gets His Man

Encyclopaedia Brown Solves Them All

Encyclopaedia Brown Keeps the Peace

Encyclopaedia Brown Saves the Day

Encyclopaedia Brown Tracks Them Down

Encyclopaedia Brown Shows the Way

Encyclopaedia Brown Takes the Case

The Famous Five: Five on a Treasure Island

Enid Blyton

 First published: 1942

The Famous Five are the siblings Julian, Dick and Anne, their cousin George (short for Georgina) and her dog Timmy. This is the first book of one of the best-selling children's series in the world.

Despite an awkward first meeting, the four children are soon friends. And when there is a shipwreck off Kirrin Island, they set out to find the treasure together.

About the author
See Part II: Humour

Read more about the Famous Five

Read about the Secret Seven

The Secret Seven

Secret Seven Adventure

Well Done, Secret Seven

Secret Seven on the Trail

Go Ahead, Secret Seven

Good Work, Secret Seven

Secret Seven Win Through

Three Cheers, Secret Seven

Secret Seven Mystery

Puzzle for the Secret Seven

Secret Seven Fireworks

Good Old Secret Seven

Shock for the Secret Seven

Look Out, Secret Seven

Fun for the Secret Seven

Read about the adventures of Jack, Lucy-Ann, Philip, Dinah and Kiki the Parrot in the Adventure series

The Island of Adventure

The Castle of Adventure

The Valley of Adventure

The Sea of Adventure

The Mountain of Adventure

The Ship of Adventure

The Circus of Adventure

The River of Adventure

Read about the adventures of Roger, Diana, Snubby and Barney in the 'R' series

The Rockingdown Mystery

The Rilloby Fair Mystery

The Ring O' Bells Mystery

The Rubadub Mystery

The Rat-a-tat Mystery

The Ragamuffin Mystery

Read about the adventures of Peggy, Mike, Nora, Jack and Prince Paul in the Secret series

The Secret Island

The Secret of Spiggy Holes

The Secret Mountain

The Secret of Killimooin

The Secret of Moon Castle

Read about the Five Find-outers

From the Mixed-Up Files of Mrs. Basil E. Frankweiler

E.L. Konigsburg

First published: 1967

Claudia Kincaid is almost twelve, bright and the eldest child in a family of four. So when such a smart child plans to run away from her family, she chooses a place that is beautiful, comfortable and preferably indoors. She plans the trip carefully, and recruits her middle brother James to be her companion. Claudia and James hide away in the Metropolitan Museum of Art for a whole week. Wandering the museum, they learn many new things and are fascinated by a new exhibit, a marble angel that may just be a genuine Michelangelo sculpture. Though time and money are both running out for the runaways, Claudia decides to solve the mystery of the angel and track down Mrs Basil E. Frankweiler, the former owner of the angel.

About the author

American author E.L. Konigsburg (b.1930) has won the Newbury award twice.

Read more by Konigsburg

Jennifer, Hecate, Macbeth, William McKinley, and Me, Elizabeth

About the B'nai Bagels George

Altogether, One at a Time

153

Stormbreaker

Anthony Horowitz

First published: 2000

Fourteen-year-old Alex Rider is devastated when he receives news of the death of his uncle, who is also his guardian, and subsequently discovers that his uncle was a spy for Britain's M16.

But soon Alex himself is recruited by the M16 to investigate the case of Herod Sayle, who has invented a new supercomputer called Stormbreaker, which he wants to distribute to schoolchildren throughout Britain. And Alex discovers that Sayle also has connections with the man who killed his uncle.

About the author

Anthony Horowitz (b.1955) is a British writer who has written TV scripts for many detective serials. His books for children include the Diamond Brothers series.

Read more about Alex Rider

Point Blanc	*Scorpia*
Skeleton Key	*Ark Angel*
Eagle Strike	

Read about the Diamond Brothers

The Falcon's Malteser	*South by South East*
Just Ask for Diamond	*The French Confection*
Public Enemy Number Two	*I Know What You Did Last Wednesday*

The Stratemeyer Syndicate and mystery stories

Edward Stratemeyer, the writer of novels and stories, set up the Stratemeyer Syndicate around 1905. He realized that he had more ideas for stories than the time to write them. Therefore, he began generating ideas for books, which would then be written by ghost writers. Some of the most popular series produced by the syndicate include the Bobbsey Twins ('by Laura Lee Hope'), Hardy Boys ('by Franklin W. Dixon') and Nancy Drew ('by Carolyn Keene').

Most of the early Hardy Boys books were written by Leslie McFarlane, a Canadian journalist. Mildred Wart Benson wrote the early Nancy Drew stories, and Harriet S. Adams (Stratemeyer's daughter who took charge of the syndicate after his death), several of the later ones.

Over the years, the series have been updated and revised. Part of the reason was because the early books were felt to be too dated for modern readers—after all, the first Nancy Drew book was published in 1930 and the first Hardy Boys book in 1927! The plots of many of the books have also been changed considerably, though the titles are still the same.

The Secret of the Old Clock
Carolyn Keene

First published: 1930
The young American detective, who lives in the
town of River Heights with her father, a lawyer, and
housekeeper, has to contend with a gang of thieves
and find an old will which is hidden in the clock.

Nancy Drew Mystery Stories Series I: fifty-six books, including

The Hidden Staircase
The Bungalow Mystery
The Mystery at Lilac Inn
The Secret at Shadow Ranch
The Secret of Red Gate Farm
The Clue in the Diary
The Sign of the Twisted Candles
The Clue of the Broken Locket
The Whispering Statue
The Haunted Bridge

Other Nancy Drew series:
Nancy Drew Mystery Stories Series II: 132 books
Nancy Drew Files: 124 books
Nancy Drew on Campus: 25 books
Nancy Drew Girl Detective: 12 books to date
The Nancy Drew Notebooks: 65 books
The Nancy Drew Graphic Novels: 3 books to date

The Tower Treasure

Franklin W. Dixon

The brothers Frank and Joe Hardy are amateur detectives. In this, the first mystery, they chase the thieves who have stolen a friend's car, uncover a thief's disguise and hunt for the treasure in the garden of the Tower mansion.

Hardy Boys Mystery Stories Series I: fifty-eight books, including

The Secret of the Old Mill

The Shore Road Mystery

The Secret of the Caves

The Mystery of Cabin Island

While the Clock Ticked

Footprints under the Window

The Mark on the Door

The Hidden Harbour Mystery

The Sinister Signpost

A Figure in Hiding

The Secret Warning

The Twisted Claw

The Disappearing Floor

The Mystery of the Flying Express

Mystery of the Chinese Junk

Mystery of the Desert Giant

The Clue of the Screeching Owl

The Viking Symbol Mystery

The Mystery of the Aztec Warrior

Danger on Vampire Trail

The Masked Monkey

The Jungle Pyramid

The Firebird Rocket

The Sting of the Scorpion

Other Hardy Boys series:
Hardy Boys Mystery Stories Series II: 132 books
The Hardy Boys Casefiles: 127 books
The Hardy Boys: The Clues Brothers: 17 books
to date
The Hardy Boys: Undercover Brothers: 7 books
to date
The Hardy Boys Graphic Novels: 3 books to date

There is also a series of thirty-six books, where Nancy Drew and the Hardy Boys join forces to combat evil. These are known as the Nancy Drew and Hardy Boys Supermysteries.

Read more in the genre

CAM JANSEN AND THE MYSTERY OF THE STOLEN DIAMONDS | DAVID A. ADLER
First book in a series of over twenty about the girl detective Cam Jansen. There is also a Cam Jansen series for younger readers.

CHASING VERMEER | BLUE BALLIETT
When a Vermeer painting disappears on its way to a museum, twelve-year-olds Petra Andalee and Calder Pillay decide to track down the thief.

EMIL AND THE DETECTIVES | ERIC KASTNER
A young boy is travelling to visit his grandmother in Berlin when he is robbed. He then decides to track down the culprits.

KRISTY'S GREAT IDEA | ANN M. MARTIN
This is the first book in the Babysitters' Club Mysteries series. There are over a hundred books in the series, in addition to which there are spin-off series and specials.

THE CHAMELEON WORE CHARTREUSE | BRUCE HALE
This is the first in the series of Chet Gecko mysteries, which combine humour, adventure and a cast of animals.

THE SECRET OF TERROR CASTLE | ROBERT ARTHUR
The three investigators—Jupiter Jones, Bob Andrews and Pete Genshaw—are friends with Alfred Hitchcock, who makes an appearance in each book. In this book, the first of the series, the three boys explore a haunted house in the hope that Hitchcock will use it for an upcoming film.

THE SECRET OF THE MANSION | JULIE CAMPBELL
First in a series of thirty-nine books about the freckled
Trixie Belden, a girl detective.

THE THIEVES OF OSTIA | CAROLINE LAWRENCE
Set in the Roman port city of Ostia in AD 79, this is
the adventure of Flavia Gemina, an amateur detective
and the daughter of a sea captain, and her three friends.
The other books in the series include *The Pirates of
Pompeii* and *The Secrets of Vesuvius*.

THE WESTING GAME | ELLEN RASKIN
The sixteen residents of Sunset Towers have to figure
out who killed Samuel Westing in order to inherit his
vast fortune.

Asterix the Gaul

René Goscinny and Albert Uderzo (illustrations)

First published: 1961

It is 50 BC and Gaul is divided into three parts under the Romans—or rather four, for one small village still holds out against the Roman invaders. Centurion Crismus Bonus is keen to discover the secret of the Gauls' superhuman strength and sends a spy into the village. Though the spy's identity is revealed when he loses his false moustaches, he has already found out about the magic potion brewed by the Druid Getafix that gives the Gauls their superior strength. The next stage for the wily Romans is to kidnap Getafix …

This is the first in a brilliant series of comic books about the exploits of Asterix and his friends, Getafix, Obelix and Cacofonix.

About the author

René Goscinny (1926–77) was a French author and humorist. He collaborated with Albert Uderzo (b.1927) for the first twenty-four books. After his death, Uderzo continued on his own, though the covers still mention both names.

Read more about Asterix

Carrie's War

Nina Bawden

 First published: 1993

During World War II, Carrie and her brother Nick are evacuated to a Welsh mining town. They live with the grocer Mr Evan and his timid sister, who the children call Auntie Lou.

Mr Evan's other sister Dilys Gotobed lives at Druid's Bottom, with her housekeeper Hepzibah Green. When the children first go there, they meet another evacuee, Albert Sandwich. Carrie loves being at Druid's Bottom—until she does something truly terrible ...

About the author

Nina Bawden (b.1925) is an award–winning British author who has written over forty books for adults and children.

Read more by Bawden

The Finding
The Peppermint Pig
Granny the Pag
A Handful of Thieves
The Secret Passage

The Outside Child
Rebel on a Rock
The Witch's Daughter
Devil by the Sea

Eagle of the Ninth
Rosemary Sutcliff

First published: 1954
The Ninth Legion marched into the mists of northern
Britain. And they are never seen again. Four thousand
men disappear and the eagle standard is lost.

Marcus Aquila's father had led the Ninth Legion.
He has to find out what happened to his father, and
sets out with his friend, the freed slave Esca, into the
unknown on a quest so hazardous that no one expects
him to return.

About the author
The award-winning British writer Rosemary Sutcliff
(1920–92) wrote over forty books, many of them
historical novels for children.

Read more about Marcus
The Silver Branch   *The Lantern Bearers*

Read more by Sutcliff
Black Ships Before Troy   *Outcast*
The Wanderings of   *The Shield Ring*
   Odysseus   *Warrior Scarlet*
The Chronicles of Robin   *Beowulf*
   Hood   *The Mark of the Horse Lord*

The Narayanpur Incident

Shashi Deshpande

First published: 1995
The story is set against the backdrop of the Quit India
movement of 1942. Babu and Manju find that their
life changes dramatically. Their school is shut down
and their father is imprisoned. Their brother Mohan
goes underground.

   The rest of the family moves to Narayanpur, a quiet
little village that seems untouched by the political
upheavals. But Narayanpur is also seething and it all
comes to a head when a group of children dare to
confront the police ...

About the author
Shashi Deshpande (b.1938) is the award-winning author
of several novels for adults.

Read more by Deshpande
   A Summer Adventure   *The Only Witness*
   The Hidden Treasure

The Diary of a Young Girl

Anne Frank

First published (in Dutch): 1947

This book is not fiction, but a true diary. Anne Frank was eleven when the Nazi German army invaded the Netherlands in 1940. There were increasingly restrictive measures taken again Jewish people. As a result, Anne and her family, who were Jewish, decided to go into hiding in the back annexe of her father Otto Frank's office in Amsterdam. They were later joined in their hiding place by Mr and Mrs Daan, their son Peter, and Mr Drussel.

Throughout the period of more than two years that thirteen-year-old Anne and her family were in hiding, Anne maintained her diary. In this she describes their daily life at the annexe—the isolation and the fear of discovery.

This book is a moving testament to the human spirit and vividly gives an eyewitness's account of one of the worst times that the world has ever known.

About the author

Anne Frank (1929–45) was a German–Jewish girl whose family had moved to the Netherlands for safety after the Nazis came to power.

Anne died at the concentration camp at Bergen Belsen.

With Clive in India

G.A. Henty

First published: 1884

Charlie Marryat, who loves adventure, is thrilled to get a job as a writer in the East India Company. However, he finds more adventure than he had anticipated when he is recruited by Clive in his campaigns to defeat the French and establish British power over India.

Charlie distinguishes himself in a number of battles and earns a reputation for courage and ingenuity. Among his many adventures, he rescues Ada Haines from an Indian harem. After ten years in India, he returns to England a wealthy man as a result of his services to a number of Indian princes.

About the author

English novelist G.A. Henty (1832–1902) wrote over a hundred historical novels for children.

Read more by Henty

At the Point of a Bayonet: A Tale of the Mahratta War

Bonnie Prince Charlie: A Tale of Fontenoy and Culloden

The Boy Knight: A Tale of the Crusade

By Conduct and Courage: A Story of the Days of Nelson

The Dragon and the Raven: The Days of King Alfred

The Fall of Sebastopol

A Final Reckoning: A Tale of Bush Life in Australia

Read more in the genre

A SINGLE SHARD | LINDA SUE PARK

Set in twelfth-century Korea, this is the story of how a single shard from a celadon vase changes the life of a young boy and his master.

AGAIN THE BUGLES BLOWS | RONALD LEONARD BACON

A gripping story of the courage of the Maoris.

CRISPIN: THE CROSS OF LEAD | AVI

An action-packed historical narrative that follows the frantic flight of a thirteen-year-old peasant boy across fourteenth-century England.

HANS BRINKER OR THE SILVER SKATES | MARY MAPES DODGE

The classic story of the boy who saved Holland from flooding.

KARTIK'S WAR | SUBHADRA SENGUPTA

Kartik is a spy in Ashoka's empire who is upset at the king's adoption of non-violence. But then he tumbles upon a conspiracy to kill the king. Read also *Bishnu Sings Again* and *The Sword of Dara Shikoh*.

LITTLE HOUSE IN THE BIG WOODS | LAURA INGALLS WILDER

The family saga of Laura, her parents, Mary and Baby Carrie in the woods of Wisconsin in the late nineteenth century. The series continues with *Little House on the Prairie, Farmer Boy, On the Banks of Plum Creek, By the Shores of Silver Lake, The Long Winter, Little Town on the Prairie, These Happy Golden Years* and *The First Four Years*.

MASTER SKYLARK: A STORY OF SHAKESPEARE'S TIME |
JOHN BENNETT
A young singer is kidnapped and taken to London
where he eventually sings for the queen.

THE MIDWIFE'S APPRENTICE | KAREN CUSHMAN
When Jane the midwife takes a nameless orphan (whom
she names Beetle) to be her apprentice, she transforms
the young girl's life. Read also *Catherine, Called Birdy*
and *Matilda Bone*.

STEAL AWAY | JENNIFER ARMSTRONG
Two thirteen-year-old girls, one black and one white,
run away from their homes and slavery in nineteenth-
century America.

THE CHINA COIN | ALLAN BAILLIE
A story a Chinese–Australian girl and Tiananmen
Square.

THE DOLPHIN CROSSING | JILL PATON WALSH
Pat and John know the risks in taking a boat across
the English Channel in the spring of 1940, but
they must help the British soldiers stuck at Dunkirk.

THE MACHINE GUNNERS | ROBERT WESTALL
Chas McGill finds a working machine gun from a
downed German plane during World War II and decides
to fight the Germans himself. The sequel is called
Fathom Five.

THE PARKHURST BOYS | MARGARET BEAMES
The story of convict apprentices sent to New Zealand
in 1842.

THE WARDEN'S NIECE | GILLIAN AVERY
Maria's adventures in nineteenth-century Oxford.

THE WHEEL OF SURYA | JAMILA GAVIN
Marvinder and Jaspal are separated from their mother as they flee their village in Punjab during the violence following Partition. Their only relative is their unknown father in England, and it is to him that they have to travel. The sequels are *The Eye of the Horse* and *The Track of the Wind*.

TOLIVER'S SECRET | ESTHER WOOD BRADY
A young girl has to be the messenger for George Washington, and carry his message through the British lines.

VIKING'S DAWN | HENRY TREECE
Harald Sigurdson is a young boy who sails with his father from the western fjords of Norway to find gold in Britain. But when his father is injured, it leaves Harald on his own. The sequels are *The Road to Miklagard* and *Viking's Sunset*.

WHEN HITLER STOLE PINK RABBIT | JUDITH KERR
Anna is nine and Jewish, and does not pay too much attention to the posters of Hitler appearing all around in Berlin. But when her father goes missing, Anna's mother decides it is time to take her children out of Germany.

WITH NOTHING BUT OUR COURAGE | KARLEEN BRADFORD
Tale of a family loyal to England after the defeat in the Revolutionary War. Read also *The Nine Days Queen* and *The Other Elizabeth*.

Lionboy
Zizou Corder

First published: 2003

Young Charlie Ashanti is unusual in many ways. His parents are scientists, he suffers from asthma, there are many cats in their house—and Charlie can speak Cat.

When Charlie comes home one day to find his parents missing and a neighbourhood hoodlum Rafi trying to draw him away, he runs away. He finds himself on perhaps the most amazing ship that ever sailed—a floating circus. Charlie has to make a place for himself in the circus, and at the same time he has to track down his parents, a task in which he is aided by his extraordinary ability to talk to cats.

About the author

The mother and daughter team of Louisa Young and Isabel Adomakoh Young write together under the name of Zizou Corder.

Read more about Lionboy

Lionboy: *The Chase*

Mr. Galliano's Circus

Enid Blyton

First published: 1938
Jimmy Brown is overjoyed when the circus comes to his town. He visits the circus every day and soon is friends with Lotta—the girl who rides the horses, Lilliput, the man with the monkeys, Stanley the clown and Mr Tonks, who is the owner of Jumbo the elephant.

One night, there is a thunderstorm which frightens Jumbo into running away. It is Jimmy who rescues him and brings him back. The following day, Mr Galliano asks Jimmy and his family to join the circus.

About the author
See Part II: Humour

Read more about Jimmy
Hurrah for the Circus   *Come to the Circus*
Circus Days Again

Swallows and Amazons

Arthur Ransome

First published: 1930

The book is set in the English Lake District in the period between the two World Wars. When the Walker children—John, Susan, Titty and Roger—are allowed to go sailing in the *Swallow* and to camp on an island, that seems adventure enough. But they soon find themselves under attack from the fierce Amazon pirates, Nancy and Peggy Blackett. And thus begins a summer of battles, alliances and discovery.

A charmingly told story with great detail about sailing and camping and the countryside lovingly described, this series has been a favourite for over seventy years.

About the author

British author Arthur Ransome (1884–1967) worked as a journalist before becoming a full-time writer. He lived in the Lake District, where this series is set.

Read more about the Swallows and Amazons

Swallowdale

Peter Duck

Winter Holiday

Coot Club

Pigeon Post

We Didn't Mean to Go to Sea

Secret Water

The Big Six

Missee Lee

The Picts and the Martyrs

Great Northern?

The Camels Are Coming
Captain W.E. Johns

 First published: 1932

The adventures of James Bigglesworth and his friends in the early days of the Royal Flying Corps during World War I.

In this collection of short stories, Biggles shoots down the elusive White Fokker which has killed one of his men, retrieves a packet on an impossible mission, kills a German pilot who is shooting down unsuspecting British pilots in a British plane and captures a German balloon. He also finds a German gun disguised as a church, rescues a spy, foils a potential German attack, gets lost in fog and meets the love of his life, Marie Janis.

About the author

Captain W.E. Johns (1893–1968) was a machine gunner and with the Royal Flying Corps during World War I. He wrote ninety-eight books on Biggles and 167 books in all.

Read more about Biggles

The Cruise of the Condor
Biggles of the Camel Squadron
Biggles Flies Again
The Black Peril
Biggles Flies East
Biggles Hits the Trail

Biggles in Africa
Biggles: Air Commodore
Biggles Goes to War
Biggles: Secret Agent
Biggles in the Baltic
Biggles in the South Seas
Biggles: Air Detective

The Red Sea Sharks

Hergé

 First published: 1956

Tintin the intrepid journalist with the uncanny ability to land in trouble is the hero of Hergé's much-loved comic strip. In this, the nineteenth adventure, the story begins with the son of the Emir of Khemed staying with Captain Haddock to improve his English. Meanwhile, a lost wallet enables Tintin to overhear sinister mentions of arms deals.

When there is a coup in Khemed, Tintin and Captain Haddock go to rescue the Emir. Tintin suspects that there is a connection between the rebel victory and the arms deal that he had heard about. His attempts to confirm this leads to much danger …

About the author

Hergé (Georges Remi) (1907–1983) was a Belgian comics writer and artist. He wrote twenty-four adventures of Tintin.

Read more about Tintin

The Black Island
The Calculus Affair
The Castafiore Emerald
Cigars of the Pharaoh
The Crab with the Golden
  Claws

Destination Moon
Land of Black Gold
Red Rackham's Treasure
Tintin and the Picaros
Tintin in Tibet

Adventure Stories

Arup Kumar Dutta

The Kaziranga Trail: First published: 1978
This collection of four action-packed stories includes
The Kaziranga Trail, *Trouble at Kolongijan*, *The Blind
Witness* and *Smack*. In *Kaziranga Trail*, three bright
teenaged village boys, Dhanai, Bubul and Jonti, along
with their young elephant Makhoni, encounter rhino
poachers in the Kaziranga sanctuary. *The Blind Witness*
is the story of Ramu, the blind—and only—witness
to a murder, who helps the police nab a gang of dreaded
smugglers, using his sharp senses. In *Trouble at Kolongijan*,
two youngsters, Moina and Ponakan, foil the avaricious
Barua's plans that would endanger the entire village.
In *Smack*, Gulu the boy waiter and Ravi, a shoeshine
boy, help bust a drug racket.

About the author
Arup Kumar Dutta (b. 1946) was born in Jorhat, Assam,
and worked as a professor of English. He writes for
both children and adults, besides working as a journalist.
His books for children have been translated into many
foreign languages and *The Blind Witness* has been
brought out in Japanese Braille.

Read more by the author
  The Brahmaputra

Read more in the genre

AMAZON ADVENTURE | WILLARD PRICE
Hal and Rodger Hunt travel to the Amazon with their father, a famous naturalist. The adventures of the brothers in quest of other animals is continued in *Whale Adventure, Gorilla Adventure, Safari Adventure, Diving Adventure* and *Elephant Adventure*, among others.

ANDAMAN: THE JARAWA | DEEPAK DALAL
A gripping tale of three children who walk into an adventure in the little-known islands. The sequel is *Andaman: Barren Island*. Read also *Ranthambore Adventure, Lakshadweep, Ladakh* and *The Snow Leopard*.

ANDAMANS BOY | ZAI WHITAKER
Tired of life in Mumbai, Arif runs away to the Andaman islands.

CAPTAIN GREY | AVI
When the murderous Captain Grey tries to wreak havoc along the New Jersey coast, only one boy called Kevin stands in his way.

HUNT FOR THE MIRACLE HERB | DEEPA AGARWAL
Uncle Raj and his mysterious companion are in search of an elusive herb which is supposed to possess amazing powers.

NO GUN FOR ASMIR | CHRISTOBEL MATTINGLEY
The story of the escape from Bosnia of seven-year-old Asmir. The sequels are *Asmir in Vienna* and *Escape from Sarajevo*.

PIPPI LONGSTOCKING | ASTRID LINDGREN
The delightful adventures of nine-year-old, carrot-topped Pippi who lives in Villa Villekulla. The

sequels include *Pippi Goes on Board* and *Pippi in the South Seas*.

THE BIG WAVE | PEARL S. BUCK
The tale of two Japanese friends whose village is swamped by a tidal wave.

TRAVELLING COMPANIONS | MARGARET BHATTY
The tale of a young boy who is drawn to life in a circus. But after a fire destroys part of the circus, the lives of the performers change for ever.

THE WIND ON THE MOON | ERIC LINKLATER
Dinah and Dorinda stage an escape from the local zoo and head off to rescue their father, accompanied by a golden puma and a silver falcon.

Cirque du Freak: A Living Nightmare

Darren Shan

First published: 2001

When Darren and his friends find a flier for a travelling freak show promising a snake boy, a wolf man, and Larten Crepsley and his giant spider Madame Octa, they decide to go along.

The show is memorable. A werewolf bites off someone's hand in the audience. Darren's friend Steve recognizes Larten to be a famous vampire and decides to join him. Darren plans to steal Madame Octa and teach her tricks in his room. And this is only the beginning of their introduction to the world of vampires, told in first person.

About the author

Darren Shan (Darren O'Shaughnessy) (b.1972) was a TV scriptwriter and is at present a full-time writer.

Read more by Darren Shan

The Vampire's Assistant   Allies of the Night
Tunnels of Blood   Killers of the Dawn
The Vampire Mountain   The Lake of Souls
The Trials of Death   Lord of the Shadows
The Vampire Prince   Sons of Destiny
Hunters of the Dusk

Complete Poems and Stories
Edgar Allan Poe

First published: 1902

Edgar Allan Poe's stories do not deal with murderers, monsters or devils—often the terrifying element simply comes from within you. Some are classic tales of detection. But what is indisputable is the fear they evoke.

Some of the best known in this collection are: 'The Murder in the Rue Morgue', 'The Golden Bug', 'The Cask of Amontillado', 'The Pit and the Pendulum' and 'The Black Cat'.

About the author

Edgar Allan Poe (1808–49) was the American master of horror and crime stories.

Coraline
Neil Gaiman

First published: 2002

Coraline and her parents live in one part of a huge house. Among the other people in the house are the former actresses Miss Spink and Miss Forcible and their aging Highland terriers, and an old man with moustaches who lives under the roof. Coraline spends days exploring the vast grounds, and when it rains, the house. At the fourteenth door, she comes across an alternative universe which corrects everything that is wrong with her present life: people pronounce her name correctly, all meals are delicious, and her bedroom is pink and green (not like her dull one). Her parents in this world look exactly like her parents in the other, except that they have big, shiny, black button eyes and paper-white skin—and they are determined to keep her on their side of the door.

About the author

Neil Gaiman (b.1960) is the creator of the Sandman series of graphic novels. He is British but currently lives in the US.

Read more by Gaiman

  Good Omens (with Terry Pratchett)

Roald Dahl's Book of Ghost Stories

First published: 1983
Roald Dahl has always been a connoisseur of the
unexpected. The fourteen stories in this collection are
spooky and disturbing. They include stories by E.F.
Benson, J. Sheridan Le Fanu, Rosemary Timperley and
Edith Wharton.

About the author
See Part II: Humour

Read more by Dahl
Tales of the Unexpected   *More Tales of the Unexpected*

Uncanny!

Paul Jennings

 First published: 1989

A collection of delightfully humorous and weirdly spooky short stories, which feature strange adventures such as going inside a dead whale, turning into a dung beetle, catching someone else's tattoos and seeing a flying dog. Includes the stories 'On the Bottom', 'A Good Tip for Ghosts', 'Frozen Stiff', 'UFD', 'Cracking Up', 'Greensleeves', 'Mousechap', 'Spaghetti Pig-Out' and 'Know All'.

About the author

Australian author Paul Jennings (b.1943) was a teacher for many years before he became a full-time writer.

Read more by Jennings

Unreal!	*The Gizmo*
Unbelievable!	*The Gizmo Again*
Round the Twist	*The Cabbage Patch Fib*
Unmentionable!	*The Cabbage Patch War*
Unbearable!	*The Paw Thing*
Wicked!	*Singenpoo Strikes Again*
Quirky Tails	*Singenpoo Shoots Through*
Undone!	*Thirteen Unpredictable Tales*
Unseen!	

Welcome to Dead House

R.L. Stine

First published: 1992

Amanda and Josh are not too happy about moving into an old haunted house located in the strange town of Dark Falls. The people in the town seem unlike people they have known before.

But after they move in, things get even stranger. Things happen that their parents cannot see—ghostly shapes at the window, their dog's reaction to strangers, shadows on the wall, and the strange death-pale children of the neighbours. Was it only the chemical spill that made the people so strange, or was it something far more sinister?

About the author

R.L. Stine (b.1943) is the author of many children's and young adult horror stories, the best known of which is the Goosebumps series, comprising over sixty books. He also writes joke books and comic books.

Read more in the Goosebumps series

Stay Out of the Basement
Monster Blood
Say Cheese and Die!
Welcome to Camp Nightmare

Be Careful What You Wish For
Why I'm Afraid of Bees
The Scarecrow Walks at Midnight

Read more in this genre

FULL TILT | NEAL SHUSTERMAN
Sixteen–year–old Blake has to experience seven wild rides before dawn to save his brother.

GHOST STORIES OF AN ANTIQUARY | M.R. JAMES
Classic collection of spooky tales.

THE BEASTIES | WILLIAM SLEATOR
The tale of the bloodthirsty creatures who need human blood to survive.

THE CALL OF CTHULHU AND OTHER WEIRD STORIES | H.P. LOVECRAFT
Includes such classic spooky stories as 'Rats in the Walls', 'Herbert West Reanimator' and 'The Haunter of the Dark'.

THE GHOST OF THOMAS KEMP | PENELOPE LIVELY
While renovating their country cottage, the Harrison family breaks a glass bottle and lets out a three–hundred–year–old spirit.

THE RUPA BOOK OF HAUNTED HOUSES | EDITED BY RUSKIN BOND
Contains classic tales from Arthur Quiller-Couch, M.R. James, E.F. Benson, Walter de la Mare and Bond.

THE SECRET PATH | CHRISTOPHER PIKE
The children of Springville rename their town Spooksville because of all the strange things that happen there. This is the first in the series of over twenty books called Spooksville.

THE THIEF OF ALWAYS | CLIVE BARKER

Harvey Swick is bored with life, and does not pause to consider the consequences when he enters Mr Hood's Holiday House.

TRAVELLER'S GHOST | DEEPA AGARWAL

There is something about Yatri's house in the little town where children have been disappearing.

Beastly Tales from Here and There
Vikram Seth

First published: 1991
Ten delightful animal tales in verse—two each from China, India, Greece and the Ukraine, and two from 'the land of Gup'. Among the old favourites is the story of Kuroop the crocodile who lives in the Ganges and his friend the monkey, and the age-old story of the hare and the tortoise ingeniously retold. There is also the amazing tale of the elephant and the tragopan, and the battle between the snake and the mouse.

The delightful versification and the strong characters give this collection its appeal.

About the author
Vikram Seth (b. 1952) is an Indian novelist and poet whose works include *The Golden Gate* (a novel in verse) and *A Suitable Boy*.

Charlotte's Web

E.B. White

First published: 1952

Wilbur, an affectionate but somewhat bashful pig, befriends a spider named Charlotte who lives in the rafters above his pen. When Wilbur discovers that he is intended to be butchered, Charlotte mounts a campaign to save his life. She spins designs on her web which show the community that Wilbur is a special animal, which subsequent events prove true ...

About the author

E.B. White (1899–1985) was an American poet, journalist and author.

Read more by White

The Trumpet of the Swan   *Stuart Little*

Mrs. Frisby and the Rats of NIMH

Robert C. O'Brien

First published: 1972

Mrs Frisby, a widowed mouse who lives with her four children at the Fitzgibbon farm, finds herself in a terrible dilemma. The farmer is going to plough the field, so she has to move, but her youngest son Timothy is very ill with pneumonia.

On the advice of the crow and the owl, Mrs Frisby approaches the rats who live nearby. Their lifestyle is most unusual—they have lifts and electric lights and they teach their young to read. They agree to help Mrs Frisby and come up with a most ingenious solution.

About the author

Robert C. O'Brien (Robert Conly) (1918–73) was a Washington-based journalist who worked for many years with the *National Geographic* magazine.

Read more about the Rats of NIMH

Racso and the Rats of NIMH (by Jane Leslie Conly)

Margaret and the Rats of NIMH (by Jane Leslie Conly)

Read more by O'Brien

The Silver Crown

Z for Zachariah

The Amazing Maurice and His Educated Rodents

Terry Pratchett

First published: 2001

The Amazing Maurice is a talking cat who has been running a brilliant scam. He has teamed up with Keith, a stupid–looking boy who happens to play a pipe, and a band of talking rats. They travel from town to town, and the townspeople pay Keith to get rid of their sudden infestation of rats.

But when they reach the town of Bad Blintz in Uberwald, there are strange things happening there. People are starving and rats have a price on their tails. The other rat catchers are killing many rats (they carry the tails as evidence) but there is not a single rat to be seen. And there is a sense that something terribly evil lurks in the cellars.

Hilarious and clever, this take on the Pied Piper story is a must-read for all Discworld fans.

About the author
See Part I: Science Fiction and Fantasy

The Hundred and One Dalmatians
Dodie Smith

First published: 1956

Pongo the Dalmatian and his wife Missis have a wonderful life. Their pets are Mr and Mrs Dearly who are gentle, obedient and unusually intelligent, and they live with Nanny Butler and Nanny Cook. Their joy seems complete when Missis has a litter of fifteen pups.

But happiness turns to horror when the pups are kidnapped, and all signs point to it being the work of Cruella de Vil, who wants a Dalmation fur coat …

About the author

Dodie Smith (1896–1990) was an actress, playwright and novelist. She and her husband had nine Dalmatians.

Read more about the Dalmatians

The Starlight Barking

See also Part I: Coming of Age

The Sheep-Pig
Dick King-Smith

First published: 1983

When Farmer Hogget wins a clever little pig called Babe in a raffle, his wife decide he will make a good Christmas dinner. However, Fly the sheepdog adopts Babe and gives him lessons in herding sheep. But Babe's techniques are somewhat different—he makes polite requests, and as a result the sheep are happy to obey.

Babe proves himself a hero when he saves the sheep from thieves. This is a new and affectionate look at life in the farmyard and the animals that live there.

About the author
Dick King-Smith (b. 1922) is a farmer in England. He started writing for children late in life.

Read more by King-Smith
Ace: The Very Important Pig
Daggie Dogfoot
The Fox Busters
Noah's Brother
Tumbleweed
Mouse Butcher
The Invisible Dog
The Schoolmouse
Harriet's Hare

Three Terrible Trins
Smasher
A Mouse Called Wolf
Harry's Mad
Martin's Mice
Spider Sparrow
The Roundhill
Mysterious Miss Slade
The Crowstarver

The Wind in the Willows

Kenneth Grahame

First published: 1908

When Mole climbs out of his hole at Mole End one day, and meanders across to the full river, he feels his life is about to change. Soon he meets up with the good natured Water Rat, the boastful Mr Toad of Toad Hall and the reclusive Badger who lives in the frightening Wild Woods, as well as a host of other creatures.

This is a classic children's story about the idyllic English countryside and riverbanks. It has been a favourite with children and adults alike for over a century.

About the author

Kenneth Grahame (1859–1932) was an English author who wrote about and for children.

Read more about Toad and his friends

Wild Wood (by Jan Needle)

The Willows in Winter (by William Horwood)

Read more in this genre

ADITI AND THE ONE-EYED MONKEY | SUNITI NAMJOSHI
A monkey, an ant and an elephant meet a princess with a mission and rally around to help her tame a dragon.

ALL CREATURES GREAT AND SMALL | JAMES HERRIOT (JAMES ALFRED WIGHT)
The hilarious adventures of a vet in Yorkshire. The sequels are *All Things Bright and Beautiful, All Things Wise and Wonderful* and *The Lord God Made Them All.*

BAMBI | FELIX SALTEN
The well-loved classic about a fawn.

BECAUSE OF WINN-DIXIE | KATE DICAMILLO
The big, ugly happy dog teaches ten-year-old Opal many lessons about life.

BHOLU AND GOLU | PANKAJ BISHT
The adventures of the circus bear and the little boy who become great friends.

BLACK BEAUTY | ANNA SEWELL
The classic autobiography of a horse who faces her worsening fortunes with bravery and fortitude.

BORN TO LEAD | PARO ANAND
The tale of a tigress rebuilding her life in a war-ravaged world.

CARBONEL: THE KING OF CATS | BARBARA SLEIGH
When Rosemary is persuaded into buying a second-hand broom and a cat she cannot afford, she has little idea that this cat is Carbonel, Prince of Royal Blood and the victim of a terrible spell.

FIRE, BED AND BONE | HENRIETTA BRANFORD
The story of a hunting dog who saves a peasant family during the revolt of 1381 in England. Read also *White Wolf*.

FOLLYFOOT | MONICA DICKENS
The first in a series of novels about Follyfoot farm, a home for retired horses.

GAY-NECK: THE STORY OF A PIGEON | DHAN GOPAL MUKERJI
The tale of a brave carrier pigeon during World War I.

JALDI'S FRIENDS | KALPANA SWAMINATHAN
The exciting adventures of a Bombay stray with ESP.

JENNIE | PAUL GALLICO
The amazing story of a boy who turns into a cat, and his friendship with a real cat. Read also *Thomasina*.

LASSIE COME HOME | ERIC KNIGHT
The classic tale of the collie seeking his old master.

MINN OF THE MISSISSIPPI | H.C. HOLLING
The tale of the turtle who travels the length of the Mississippi.

MINNIE | ANNIE SCHMIDT
Minnie (a cat who ate some contaminated food and became a girl) lives with the journalist Mr Tibbs, and supplies him with all kinds of news gathered from her feline friends.

MORA | MULK RAJ ANAND
The story of a baby elephant who must learn the skills needed to survive.

MOUSE ATTACK | MANJULA PADMA
Arvee, a white mouse from a laboratory, now has a new home with little Mo. But then he discovers that the other brown mice who live around the house are in great danger. The sequel is *Mouse Invaders*.

NATIONAL VELVET | ENID BAGNOLD
Fourteen-year-old Velvet is determined to turn her untamed horse into a champion and personally ride him to victory in the world's greatest steeplechase, the Grand National.

REDWALL | BRIAN JACQUES
Mice and other woodlawn creatures defend a monastery against an outlaw band of rats. This is the first in a series of over fifteen books.

TARKA THE OTTER | HENRY WILLIAMSON
The adventures of Tarka, born beside the river Torridge, and his journeys through North Devon.

THE ADVENTURES OF A NEPALI FROG | KANAK MANI DIXIT
The wanderings of a frog through the mountain kingdom.

THE BLACK STALLION | WALTER FARLEY
A shipwreck leaves young Alec stranded on a deserted island with his stallion. This is the first in a series of over twenty books about the black stallion.

THE CATERPILLAR WHO WENT ON A DIET AND OTHER STORIES | RANJIT LAL
Fourteen hilarious stories about the inner lives of insects. Read also *When Banshee Kissed Bimbo and Other Stories, Small Tigers of Shergarh, The Life and Times of Altu Faltu* and *That Summer at Kalagarh*.

SIX LIVES OF FANKLE THE CAT | GEORGE MACKAY BROWN
Though her mother hates cats, Jennie has to rescue Fankle and take him home, where he tells her the wonderful adventures of his past lives.

THE TALE OF DESPEREAUX | KATE DICAMILLO
When Despereaux the mouse falls in love with human Princess Pea, the consequences can only be disastrous.

THE WATER BABIES | CHARLES KINGSLEY
The magical adventures of Tom the chimneysweep in the land below water.

TIME CAT | LLOYD ALEXANDER
The adventures of Jason and his talking and time-travelling cat Gareth. Read also *The Remarkable Journey of Prince Jen*.

TIME STOPS FOR NO MOUSE | MICHAEL HOEYE
When Hermux Tantamoq, the watchmaking mouse, realizes that his beloved, the fearless aviatrix Ms Linka Perflinger, is in danger, it is time to start a new life. The sequels are *The Sands of Time* and *No Time Like Show Time*.

TOAD RAGE | MORRIS GLEITZMAN
Young Limpy cannot understand why humans hate his kind so much, and sets off to try to change their relationship. The sequel is *Toad Heaven*.

COBRA IN MY KITCHEN | ZAI WHITAKER
A stranger-than-fiction collection of stories, poems and articles about creatures great and small.

Animal stories for young adults

THE CALL OF THE WILD | JACK LONDON
Tale of survival in the frozen Alaskan Klondike.
The sequel is *White Fang.*

TALES FROM THE INDIAN JUNGLES | KENNETH ANDERSON
Anderson's tales of the jungles of south India.

MAN-EATERS OF KUMAON | JIM CORBETT
Corbett's tales of tigers in his home state of Kumaon.

WATERSHIP DOWN | RICHARD ADAMS
A warren of rabbits from Berkshire have to set off
to look for a new home when their old home is
taken over by property developers.

Billy Bunter of Greyfriars School

Frank Richards

First published: 1947

William George Bunter is known as the 'fat owl' at Greyfriars School. He purloins tuck, avoids cricket practice and is always in trouble with his teacher Mr Quelch. For all these reasons, Bunter isn't very popular with the rest of the school. The teachers don't take too well to Bunter either, because of his tendency to fall asleep in class and to translate the Latin phrase 'Caesar adsum jam forte' as 'Caesar had some jam for tea'! Their simple remedy is to punish him, but Bunter is familiar with the sharp sting of the cane. He sees no reason to reform his ways …

Bunter's classmates, the Famous Five (Harry Wharton, Bob Chemy, Johnny Bull, Frank Nugent and Huree Jamset Rana Singh) are the real heroes who have adventures and solve mysteries. Several of the books are set outside the school as well.

About the author

Billy Bunter stories were published in the British magazine *Magnet*. The idea for Bunter came from Charles Hamilton (writing as Frank Richards) (1876–1951), but some of the Bunter stories were also written by other authors writing as Richards. Hamilton's other works include the tales of Bessie Bunter of Cliff House

School (written as Hilda Richards, Frank's sister) and *Tom Merry of St. Jim's* (as Martin Clifford).

Read more about Billy Bunter

First Term at Malory Towers
Enid Blyton

First published: 1946
Darrell Rivers is not too enthusiastic about going to
Malory Towers, the famous boarding school in Cornwall.
She does not particularly like the other girls there—
and they are soon treated to a display of her famous
temper. But gradually things fall into place as she
starts to get to know the calm and collected Sally
Hope, the musically talented Irene, the artist Belinda,
Alicia who is always up to her tricks, and the quiet and
gentle Mary Lou. The teachers are equally diverse, and
there are always classroom tricks and midnight feasts
to enliven things.

About the author
See Part II: Humour
   Enid Blyton's other famous school series are the
St. Clare's series and the Naughtiest Girl series. Blyton's
second husband was called Darrell Waters, and the
heroine of the Malory Towers series could have been
named after him.

Read more about Darrell

Read about St. Clare's

Read about the Naughtiest Girl

The Naughtiest Girl series has been continued by Anne Digby, author of the Trebizon series of school stories.

Jennings Goes to School
Anthony Buckeridge

First published: 1950

Jennings is a character based on a schoolmaster's experience and observation of real boys.

Jennings and his trusty sidekick, Darbyshire have a knack for making trouble at Linbury Court School! Their spectacular schemes create havoc, but the roguish schoolboys have heaps of fun.

About the author

Anthony Buckeridge (1912–2004) went to a boarding school and was later also a schoolmaster. He wrote stories for radio and TV, as well as books.

Read more about Jennings

Jennings' Little Hut   *Thanks to Jennings*
Jennings and Darbyshire   *Take Jennings for Instance*
Jennings' Diary   *Jennings as Usual*
According to Jennings   *Trouble with Jennings*
Our Friend Jennings

Harriet the Spy
Louise Fitzhugh

First published: 1964

Harriet lives in New York. Her favourite pastime is to observe people in secret, such as the woman who never gets out of bed, the man with twenty-five cats and the Italian family at the grocery store. She then writes about them in her notebook. Her ambition is to become a spy when she grows up, and know everything in the world.

Harriet also writes notes on her friends and the people she knows. When her notebook is read by her classmates, Harriet's true opinion of them is revealed and she is ostracized by the whole class. When her parents find out, she is banned from taking notes. This is not a situation that Harriet can cope with, and she has to find a way out.

About the author
American author and painter Louise Fitzhugh (1928–74) wrote several unusual children's books.

Read more about Harriet
The Long Secret   *Sport*

Read more in the genre

A SWARM IN MAY | WILLIAM MAYNE
John Owen's adventures in the Choir School. This is the first in a series of four books.

BLUBBER | JUDY BLUME
Jill goes along with the rest of her class in bullying classmates, but when she becomes the target, she does not like it.

FIRST TERM AT TREBIZON | ANNE DIGBY
First of a fourteen-book series about the adventures of Rebecca Mason and her friends at the famous Trebizon Boarding School in Cornwall.

GOODBYE, MR. CHIPS | JAMES HILTON
The affectionate tale of Arthur Chipping, an old schoolmaster at Brookfield School.

IT HAPPENED THAT YEAR | BUBLA BASU
The book follows the adventures of Vikram, Amita, Pia, Rakesh, Dev and Rhea in Class VIII. The sequel is *Upto the Nines*.

MIKE: A PUBLIC SCHOOL STORY | P.G. WODEHOUSE
When Mike Jackson joins Wrykyn School, much fun and mayhem ensues. Wodehouse's other school stories include *The Pothunters*, *A Prefect's Uncle*, *Tales of St. Austin's*, and *The Gold Bat*.

SCHOOL SOUP | PARO ANAND
A collection of short stories about issues that affect today's school-going children in India.

SIDEWAYS STORIES FROM WAYSIDE SCHOOL | LOUIS SACHAR
The Wayside School was supposed to be one storey high, with thirty classrooms side by side. However, it

was built sideways, and so it has thirty one-classroom floors. And strange things happen in them. The series continues with *Wayside School is Falling Down* and *Wayside School Gets a Little Stranger*, as well as two books of arithmetic puzzles from Wayside School.

STALKY AND CO. | RUDYARD KIPLING
Collection of school stories set in a military boarding school.

THE ADVENTURES OF CAPTAIN UNDERPANTS | DAV PILKEY
George and Harold hypnotize their principal Mr Krupp into believing that he is a superhero who solves crimes in his underwear. First book in a series of ten.

THE NICEST GIRL IN THE SCHOOL | ANGELA BRAZIL
One of the perennially popular school stories by Brazil, who wrote over fifty books in this genre in early twentieth century England.

THE SCHOOL AT THE CHALET | ELINOR M. BRENT-DYER
First in the series of over fifty books about the school by the lake in Austria. In this book, the series starts with Joey, Grizel, Simone and six Tirolian girls as the first pupils in the school.

THIS SCHOOL IS DRIVING ME CRAZY | NAT HENTOFF
Alcott is the best school in the city, but life there is complicated for Sam as his father is the headmaster. Read also *Does This School Have Capital Punishment?*

TO SIR, WITH LOVE | E.R. BRAITHWAITE
The modern classic about a dedicated teacher in a tough London school who slowly and painfully breaks down the barriers of racial prejudice.

TOM BROWN'S SCHOOLDAYS | THOMAS HUGHES
The tale of a pre-Victorian schoolboy at Rugby.

WHAT KATY DID AT SCHOOL | SUSAN COOLIDGE
The second book in the Katy series, where Katy is sent to school at Hillsover.

See also *Malgudi Schooldays* by R.K. Narayan (Part II: Growing up), *Little Men* by Louisa May Alcott, *A Little Princess* by Frances Hodgson Burnett, and *The Chocolate War* by Robert Cormier.

101 FOLKTALES FROM INDIA | EUNICE DE SOUZA
Folktales from all parts of the country.

A SKYFUL OF STORIES | SHOBHA VISWANATH
Tales about the constellations from all around the world.
It includes stories from ancient Greece, Rome, India,
Egypt and from aboriginal, Asian and Native American
traditions.

FOLKTALES FROM INDIA | A.K. RAMANUJAN
Oral tales from twenty-two languages.

IN WORSHIP OF SHIVA | SHANTA RAMESHWAR RAO
Retelling of Indian myths and traditional tales of gods
and nagas, the netherworld and the cosmic one.

INDIAN TALES | ROMILA THAPAR
Historical tales of larger-than-life characters—heroes
and heroines, gods and demons, and of animals.

THE MAHABHARATA | SHANTA RAMESHWAR RAO
An excellent retelling of the epic for children. Also
read *The Rainmakers and Other Stories*, a masterly and
witty retelling of folk stories and legends from different
parts of the world.

MYTHOLOGY | EDITH HAMILTON
A complete introduction to western myths—Greek,
Roman and Norse.

PRINCESS BRIDE | WILLIAM GOLDMAN
A traditional fairytale turned upside down in this story
of Buttercup, Wesley the farmboy, Fezzik the gentle
giant, and the vile prince Humperdink.

RUSSIAN FAIRY TALES | ALEKSANDR AFANAS'EV
Over two hundred colourful folk and fairytales are collected in this volume, which includes stories of Vasi Lisa the Fair, Poor Ivan, Father Frost, Baga Yaga and the evil Koshchei.

TALES FROM SHAKESPEARE | CHARLES AND MARY LAMB
A collection of twenty of Shakespeare's best plays retold in prose for the younger readers, this book has now become a classic in its own right.

SEASONS OF SPLENDOUR | MADHUR JAFFREY
Internationally best-selling collection of Indian folk tales.

TALES FROM THE PANCHATANTRA | MEERA UBEROI
The classic tales retold for contemporary children.

THE ADVENTURES OF BHIM THE BOLD | MARGARET BHATTY
The adventures of the mightiest Pandava.

THE BROKEN TUSK | UMA KRISHNASWAMI
Tales of Ganesha.

THE RAMAYANA FOR CHILDREN | BULBUL SHARMA
The epic retold for middle readers.

THE LITTLE BOOKROOM | ELEANOR FARJEON
Twenty-six delightful stories of princes, commoners, painters, dancers and goldfish.

UNCLE REMUS: HIS SONGS AND HIS SAYINGS | JOEL CHANDLER HARRIS
Classic stories of Brer Fox, Brer Rabbit and others.

Perhaps the most popular introduction to the traditional tales of India is the Amar Chitra Katha series which has an extensive collection of tales from the epics, Puranas and mythological tales.

PART III

Younger Readers

The Story of Babar

Jean de Brunhoff (text and illustrations)

First published (in French): 1931

When Babar the little elephant loses his mother, he wanders into the city, gets a new wardrobe and becomes part of high society. But in the end, he is happy to go home to his friends and family, where he is eventually crowned king of elephants.

About the author

Jean de Brunhoff (1899–1937) was a French painter and writer. The series was continued by his son Laurent de Brunhoff. An animation series has been made from the series.

Read more about Babar

Babar and Father Christmas   Babar and His Children
Babar and Zephir   The Travels of Babar
Babar the King

The Tale of Peter Rabbit
Beatrix Potter (text and illustrations)

 First published: 1902

When Mrs Rabbit goes out shopping, she warns her four children Flopsy, Mopsy, Cottontail and Peter not to go into Mr McGregor's garden. But of course that is the first place where Peter goes—and eats lettuce, French beans and radishes. But then he is spotted by Mr McGregor …

About the author

Beatrix Potter (1866–1943) spent most of her life in the Lake District in England, where these stories are set. The original twenty-three books have now been made into animation series, and there are many spin-off books.

Read more about Peter Rabbit and his friends

The Tale of Squirrel Nutkin
The Tailor of Gloucester
The Tale of Benjamin Bunny
The Tale of Mrs. Tiggy-Winkle
The Tale of the Pie and the Patty-Pan
The Tale of Mr Jeremy Fisher
The Story of a Fierce Bad Rabbit
The Story of Miss Moppet
The Tale of Tom Kitten
The Tale of Jemima Puddle-Duck

Mr Bump

Roger Hargreaves (text and illustrations)

 First published: 1971

Poor Mr Bump is very clumsy. He is always bumping into everything, and he can't keep a job because he is always breaking things. This is the story of all the jobs he has had and how he finally discovers what he is best at.

About the author

Roger Hargreaves (1935–88) created a total of forty-three Mr Men books and thirty Little Miss books. The series have been continued by his son Adam Hargreaves, and there have been many spin-off titles.

Read more in the Mr Men and Little Miss series

Mr Tickle	*Little Miss Neat*
Mr Greedy	*Little Miss Sunshine*
Mr Happy	*Little Miss Tiny*
Mr Nosey	*Little Miss Trouble*
Mr Sneeze	*Little Miss Giggles*
Mr Snow	*Little Miss Helpful*
Mr Messy	*Little Miss Magic*
Mr Topsy-Turvy	*Little Miss Shy*
Mr Silly	*Little Miss Splendid*
Mr Fussy	
Mr Bounce	
Mr Muddle	

Winnie-the-Pooh

A.A. Milne (illustrated by Ernest H. Shepard)

First published: 1926

These are the magical tales of Christopher Robin and Winnie the Pooh, the bear of very little brain, and their friends Eeyore, Piglet, Kanga and Roo, who live in the Hundred Acre Woods. In this book, Pooh and Piglet nearly catch a woozle, Eeyore loses a tail and Pooh finds one, and Piglet meets a Heffalump, among many other stories.

About the author

A.A. Milne (1882–1956) was a playwright and journalist. There have been several films and animation series based on Pooh, and several spin-off books.

Read more about Pooh and his friends

The House at Pooh Corner (illustrated by Shepard)

When We Were Very Young (illustrated by Shepard)

Now We Are Six (illustrated by Shepard)

The Cat in the Hat

Dr Seuss (text and illustrations)

First published: 1957

On a cold wet afternoon, the narrator and his sister Sally have nothing to do while their mother is out. As they sit and watch the rain, the Cat in the Hat arrives. He proceeds to entertain them by holding up the fishbowl, a toy ship, a cake, a cup and a book while standing on a ball. When the fish protests, he brings in Thing 1 and Thing 2. By now, the house is a mess and their mother is on her way home …

About the author

Dr Seuss (Theodor Seuss Geisel) (1904–91) was an American cartoonist and writer, best known for his children's books.

Read more by Seuss

Green Eggs and Ham
And to Think that I Saw It on Mulberry Street
The 500 Hats of Bartholomew Cubbins
Horton Hatches the Egg
How the Grinch Stole Christmas!
The Lorax
Yertle the Turtle and Other Stories

Tiger on a Tree
Anushka Ravishankar (illustrated by Pulak Biswas)

First published: 1997

A curious tiger swims across a river and roams the forest looking for adventure. But frightened by the cry of a small animal, he climbs a tree where a group of men from a village find him. They decide to capture him, but have no idea what to do with him after that. The whimsical poem by Anushka Ravishankar is matched by Pulak Biswas's bold artwork in black and orange.

About the author
Anushka Ravishankar is the award-winning author of several books for children.

Read more by Ravishankar

Anything But a Grabooberry (illustrated by Rathna Ramanathan)

Catch That Crocodile! (illustrated by Pulak Biswas)

The Fivetongued Firefanged Folkadotted Dragon Snake (illustrated by Indrapramit Roy and Rathna Ramanathan)

Alphabets Are Amazing Animals (illustrated by Christiane Pieper)

One, Two, Tree! (illustrated by Durga Bai)

Today Is My Day (illustrated by Piet Grobler)

Wish You Were Here (illustrated by Trotsky Marudu)

See also Part II: Humour

Little Noddy Goes to Toyland

Enid Blyton (illustrated by Harmsen van der Beek)

 First published: 1949

In the first book in the series of twenty-four, we learn how Noddy is created, how he goes to Toyland, his first meeting with Big Ears and how he gets his car and house, and makes the first few friends. There are now many spin-offs from the original Noddy books. The popularity of Noddy has led to a lot of Noddy animation films and merchandise.

About the author

See Part II: Humour

Read more about Noddy

Noddy Meets Father Christmas

Mr Plod and Little Noddy

Noddy Goes to Sea

Noddy and the Bumpy Dog

Well Done, Noddy!

Hurrah for Little Noddy

Be Brave, Little Noddy

Noddy and His Car

Do Look Out, Noddy

Noddy Goes to the Fair

Noddy Goes to School

Read more by Blyton for younger readers

Bimbo and Topsy

The Adventures of Binkle and Flip

The Adventures of Mr Pink-Whistle

Don't Be Silly, Mr Twiddle!

You're a Nuisance Mister Meddle

Fairy Tales and Stories
Hans Christian Andersen

First published (in Danish): 1835
Andersen's tales of the Little Mermaid, the Ugly
Duckling, the Emperor's New Clothes and the Princess
and the Pea, among others, are household classics around
the world.

About the author
Hans Christian Andersen (1805–75) was a Danish
author and poet.

Read more for younger readers

A BEAR CALLED PADDINGTON | MICHAEL BOND (ILLUSTRATED BY PEGGY FORTNUM)

Paddington Bear has travelled from Darkest Peru with only a jar of marmalade, a suitcase and his hat. He meets the Brown family at Paddington railway station and decides to go home with them. There are over twenty books in the series.

A CHILD'S GARDEN OF VERSES | ROBERT LOUIS STEVENSON

121 delightful and timeless poems for children.

A FLAT FOR RENT | LEAH GOLDBERG (ILLUSTRATED BY HARINDAR SINGH)

When the mouse moves out, the hen, cuckoo, squirrel and cat must find a new tenant for his flat.

A WILD ELEPHANT AT CAMP | ANUPAMA MOHORKAR (ILLUSTRATED BY EMANUELE SCANZIANI)

When an abandoned baby elephant is found in the sanctuary, Kutti becomes her caretaker and friend.

ALL FREE | MAMTA PANDYA (ILLUSTRATIONS BY SRIVIDYA NATARAJAN)

Bhikhubhai's desperate attempts to get himself a free coconut. Read also *Mazzoo Mazzoo* and *Wrestling Mania*.

BABU THE WAITER | SIRISH RAO

A day in the life of Babu the waiter in a small restaurant. Read also *Ponni the Flower Seller*.

BILLY AND BLAZE | C.W. ANDERSON (TEXT AND ILLUSTRATIONS)

Billy is a boy who loves horses more than anything. And then one day, he gets his own! This is the first in the series of Billy and Blaze books.

CHESTER'S WAY | KEVIN HENKES (TEXT AND ILLUSTRATIONS)
Chester and Wilson have their own way of doing things, but when Lily moves into the neighbourhood, all that changes.

CLASSIC INDIAN TALES FOR CHILDREN | MEERA UBEROI
A wonderfully illustrated collection of traditional Indian tales.

DINOSAURS BEFORE DARK | MARY POPE OSBORNE
Jack and Annie find a treehouse filled with books. When Jack wishes he could see the pteranodon pictured in one of them, the children are transported to the Cretaceous period. There are over thirty books in the Magic Tree series, including *The Knight at Dawn, Mummies in the Morning, Pirates Past Noon* and *Night of the Ninjas.*

EECHA POOCHA | KALA SASHIKUMAR (ILLUSTRATIONS BY ASHOK RAJAGOPAL)
Eecha the fly and Poocha the cat make rice soup together.

EKKI DOKKI | SANDHYA RAO (ILLUSTRATIONS BY RANJAN DE)
Ekkesvali, who has one hair on her head, and Dhonkesvali, who has two, meet an old woman who lives in a clearing in the middle of a forest. Read also *And Land Was Born* (illustrations by Uma Krishnaswamy).

ELOISE | KAY THOMPSON
The adventures of the six-year-old who lives in the Plaza Hotel in New York with her nanny who says everything three times, her dog Weenie, her turtle Skipperdee and two dolls. The sequels are *Eloise in*

Paris, *Eloise at Christmas time*, *Eloise in Moscow* and *Eloise Takes a Bawth*.

FLANIMALS | RICKY GERVAIS (ILLUSTRATIONS BY ROB STEEN)
Meet the Glonk, the Puddloflaj, the Plamglotis and a host of other wonderful creatures.

HEN-SPARROW TURNS PURPLE | GITA WOLF (ILLUSTRATIONS BY PULAK BISWAS)
The cheerful tale of the hen-sparrow who falls into a vat of dye. The book is designed as a scroll, and the illustrations are in the style of Indian miniature paintings. Read also *The Very Hungry Lion* (illustrations by Indrapramit Roy), an adaptation of a traditional folk tale about the lazy lion.

HISS, DON'T BITE | VAYU NAIDU (ILLUSTRATIONS BY MUGDHA SHAH)
A bad-tempered snake is taught a valuable lesson by a wandering monk. For more, you can read *A Curly Tale* (illustrations by Mugdha Shah).

HOUSEHOLD TALES | JACOB AND WILHELM GRIMM
Classic collection of folktales including 'Little Red Riding Hood', 'Rapunzel', 'Cinderella', 'The Frog Prince' and 'Hansel and Gretel'.

I AM BETTER THAN YOU | SIGRUN SRIVASTAVA
A sensitive story about sibling rivalry.

IF YOU GIVE A MOUSE A COOKIE | LAURA JOFFE NUMEROFF (ILLUSTRATIONS BY FELICIA BOND)
This might be an unexpectedly exhausting process! Other books in the series include *If You Give a Moose a Muffin*, *If You Give a Pig a Pancake* and more.

KALI AND THE RAT SNAKE | ZAI WHITAKER (ILLUSTRATIONS BY SRIVIDYA NATARAJAN)
Kali's father is a snake-catcher, and all the children in Kali's class think he is strange. But one day, things change ...

MAD MANGO | A.N. PEDNEKAR (ILLUSTRATIONS BY MANJULA PADMANABHAN)
The mango tree is bored of standing in one place and wants to see the world.

MAHARAJA RANJIT SINGH | PRITAM SINGH
A grandmother tells her grandchildren the story of the brave king of Punjab.

MAKE WAY FOR DUCKLINGS | ROBERT MCCLOSKEY (TEXT AND ILLUSTRATIONS)
Mr and Mrs Mallard think they have found the perfect spot for their ducklings in Boston's Public Garden.

MATSYA THE BEAUTIFUL FISH | SHANTA RAMESHWAR RAO (ILLUSTRATIONS BY SIGRUN SRIVASTAVA)
The story of the beautiful fish who grows up to become the saviour of mankind.

MONKEY'S DRUM | ANITA MOORTHY (ILLUSTRATIONS BY SOUMITRO SARKAR)
When Monkey gets a thorn in his tail, he asks the village barber to remove it for him. But disaster ensues.

MUTHU'S DREAM | KAMAKSHI BALASUBRAMANIAN (ILLUSTRATIONS BY TAPAS GUHA)
A young daydreamer suddenly finds out that dreams may indeed come true.

ONE DAY | JAGDISH JOSHI (TEXT AND ILLUSTRATIONS)
Mana and his friend Appu the elephant have many adventures in the jungle. For more, read *How Munia Found the Gold*.

THE PUFFIN BOOK OF BEDTIME STORIES | RUSKIN BOND ET AL
A collection of Indian bedtime stories for children.

RED KITE | GEETA DHARMARAJAN (ILLUSTRATED BY S. SEN ROY)
The red kite only dreams of flying high in the sky.

RUPA THE ELEPHANT | MICKEY PATEL (TEXT AND ILLUSTRATIONS)
Rupa the elephant only wants to look beautiful.

THE SELFISH GIANT | OSCAR WILDE
A classic story of a giant who returns home to find children playing in his garden and builds a high wall to keep them out.

SONA'S ADVENTURE | TARA TEWARI (ILLUSTRATIONS BY MICKEY PATEL)
Sona the camel is laughed at by the other animals because of her funny appearance. But later the animals come to realize how useful she is.

THE DAY I SWAPPED MY FATHER FOR 2 GOLDFISH | NEIL GAIMAN (ILLUSTRATIONS BY DAVE McKEAN)
What if you wanted your friend's goldfish so much that you swapped your father for them? Read also *Wolves in the Wall*.

THE GIVING TREE | SHEL SILVERSTEIN (TEXT AND ILLUSTRATIONS)
Once upon a time, there was a tree who loved a boy. How the tree helps the boy is the subject of this charming fable. Read also *A Giraffe and a Half* and *The Missing Piece*.

THE LITTLEST WAVE | SUMANA CHANDAVARKAR
A little girl has a special friendship with a little wave.

THE POLAR EXPRESS | CHRIS VAN ALLSBURG (TEXT AND ILLUSTRATIONS)
Santa takes a boy on a trip to the North Pole on Christmas Eve.

THE SPECTACULAR SPECTACLE MAN | VISHAKHA CHANCHANI (TEXT AND ILLUSTRATIONS)
Chashmuddin the street-spectacle seller is a man with bizarre wit.

THE STORY OF FERDINAND THE BULL | MUNRO LEAF (ILLUSTRATIONS BY ROBERT LAWSON)
Ferdinand is a gentle Spanish bull who prefers smelling flowers to butting heads. But one day when he is bitten by a bee, life changes …

THE STOWAWAY | MELANIE SEQUIERA (ILLUSTRATIONS BY HARINDER SINGH)
Marco Puss the cat wants to travel the world but is thrown off the ship. But Marco is not a cat to take this lying down …

THE SUN FAIRIES | SWAPNA DUTTA (ILLUSTRATIONS BY GEETA VADHERA)
When the sun fairies tire of their usual games and start making more and more clouds, there are unexpected consequences.

THE VELVETEEN RABBIT | MARGERY WILLIAMS (ILLUSTRATIONS BY WILLIAM NICHOLSON)
A stuffed toy rabbit comes to life through the love of his owner.

THE WINNING TEAM | GITHA HARIHARAN (ILLUSTRATIONS BY TAPOSHI GHOSHAL)
A collection of short stories that update traditional talls of wit to reveal sources of both joy and sadness in the lives of today's children.

UNDER THE MISHMASH TREE | DICK KING-SMITH

The tale of the slobbadunks and gombrizils, strollops and the long-eared spuddicks who all live together under the mishmash trees.

THE WHY-WHY GIRL | MAHASWETA DEVI (ILLUSTRATIONS BY KANYIKA KINI)

Moyna lives in a tribal village and has to work all day. But she is full of questions about everything around her.

WHERE THE WILD THINGS ARE | MAURICE SENDAK (TEXT AND ILLUSTRATIONS)

When Max gets sent to bed without supper, a forest grows in his bedroom.

WHO WILL BE NINGTHOU? | INDIRA MUKHERJEE (ILLUSTRATIONS BY A.V. ILANGO)

The king and queen of Manipur have to decide who will succeed to the throne from among their four children.

WHY ARE YOU AFRAID TO HOLD MY HAND? | SHEILA DHIR (TEXT AND ILLUSTRATIONS)

A book about the confusions and problems of a child with cerebral palsy.

INDEX BY TITLE

244

245

256